contents

Welcome to the Alan Rogers
'101' guides

The Alan Rogers guides have been helping campers and caravanners make informed decisions about their holiday destinations since 1968. Today, whether online or in print, Alan Rogers still provides an independent, impartial view, with detailed reports, on each campsite.

With so much unfiltered, unqualified information freely available, the Alan Rogers perspective is invaluable to make sure you make the right choice for your holiday.

101 best campsites

for nature lovers

2012 EDITION

alan rogers

Compiled by: Alan Rogers Guides Ltd

Designed by: Vine Design Ltd

© Alan Rogers Guides Ltd 2011

Published by: Alan Rogers Guides Ltd,
Spelmonden Old Oast, Goudhurst, Kent TN17 1HE
www.alanrogers.com
Tel: 01580 214000

British Library Cataloguing-in-Publication Data:
A catalogue record for this book is available from
the British Library.

ISBN 978-1-906215-65-1

Printed in Great Britain by
Stephens & George Print Group

What is the '101' **series**?

At Alan Rogers, we know that readers have many and diverse interests, hobbies and particular requirements. And we know that our guides, featuring a total of some 3,000 campsites, can provide a bewildering choice from which it can be difficult to produce a shortlist of possible holiday destinations.

The Alan Rogers 101 guides are devised as a means of presenting a realistic, digestible number of great campsites, featured because of their suitability to a given theme.

This book remains first and foremost an authoritative guide to excellent campsites with an emphasis on natural surroundings and where you'll be close to nature.

101 **Best campsites for nature**

More than any other form of holiday, camping is closely linked with nature. Whether you trace the links back to primitive forms of camping, such as the Native Indians or even the Scout movement, all require an understanding of our natural surroundings and a dependence on it.

Today, for most people, the main appeal of a camping holiday is that link with nature – however it may manifest itself.

We may dream wistfully of childhood tents in the garden, waking up to the dawn chorus after a night of toasted marshmallows and fireside stories. We may dream of life in the wigwams of the North American prairies, at one with nature. We may dream of taking the caravan deep into some picture postcard location, or unpacking the surfboard on some wild, unspoilt beach.

Wherever we look for nature, and whatever we want from that quest, camping 'amidst nature' invariably brings a unique sense of wellbeing and a taste of a simpler life.

This guide highlights 101 campsites which all, in differing ways, offer a taste of nature. Whether nestling in wild dunes by the sea or surrounded by alpine meadows, you'll find a campsite which will provide you with a taste of the natural world.

Alan Rogers – in search of 'the best'

Alan Rogers himself started off with the very specific aim of providing people with the necessary information to allow them to make an informed decision about their holiday destination. Today we still do that with a range of guides that now covers Europe's best campsites in 27 countries.

We work with campsites all day, every day. We visit campsites for inspection purposes (or even just for pleasure!). We know campsites 'inside out'.

We know which campsites would suit active families; which are great for get-away-from-it-all couples; we know which campsites are planning super new pool complexes; which campsites offer a fantastic menu in their on-site restaurant; which campsites allow you to launch a small boat from their slipway; which campsites have a decent playing area for kicking a ball around; which campsites have flat, grassy pitches and which have solid hard standings.

We also know which are good for fishing, golf, spas, children, nature and outdoor activities; which are close to the beach; and which welcome dogs. These particular themes form our '101' series.

All Alan Rogers guides (and our website) are respected for their independent, impartial and honest assessment. The reviews are prose-based, without overuse of indecipherable icons and symbols. Our simple aim is to help guide you to a campsite that matches best your requirements – often quite difficult in today's age of information overload.

What is the **best**?

The criteria we use when inspecting and selecting sites are numerous, but the most important by far is the question of good quality. People want different things from their choice of campsite, so campsite 'styles' vary dramatically: from small peaceful campsites in the heart of the countryside, to 'all singing, all dancing' sites in popular seaside resorts.

The size of the site, whether it's part of a chain or privately owned, makes no difference in terms of it being required to meet our exacting standards in respect of its quality and it being 'fit for purpose'. In other words, irrespective of the size of the site, or the number of facilities it offers, we consider and evaluate the welcome, the pitches, the sanitary facilities, the cleanliness, the general maintenance and even the location.

Expert opinions

We rely on our dedicated team of Site Assessors, all of whom are experienced campers, caravanners or motorcaravanners, to visit and recommend campsites. Each year they travel around Europe inspecting new campsites for Alan Rogers and re-inspecting the existing ones.

When planning
your **holiday...**

A holiday should always be a relaxing affair, and a campsite-based holiday particularly so. Our aim is for you to find the ideal campsite for your holiday, one that suits your requirements. All Alan Rogers guides provide a wealth of information, including some details supplied by campsite owners themselves, and the following points may help ensure that you plan a successful holiday.

Find out more

An Alan Rogers reference number (eg **FR 12345**) is given for each campsite and can be useful for finding more information and pictures online at www.alanrogers.com

Simply enter this number in the 'Campsite Search' field on the Home page.

Campsite descriptions

We aim to convey an idea of its general appearance, 'feel' and features, with details of pitch numbers, electricity, hardstandings etc.

Facilities

We list specific information on the site's facilities and amenities and, where available, the dates when these facilities are open (if not for the whole season). Much of this information is as supplied to us and may be subject to change. Should any particular activity or aspect of the campsite be important to you, it is always worth discussing with the campsite before you travel.

Swimming pools

Opening dates, any charges and levels of supervision are provided where we have been notified. In some countries (notably France) there is a regulation whereby Bermuda-style shorts may not be worn in swimming pools (for health and hygiene reasons). It is worth ensuring that you do take 'proper' swimming trunks with you.

Charges

Those given are the latest provided to us, usually 2011 prices, and should be viewed as a guide only.

Toilet blocks

We assume that toilet blocks will be equipped with a reasonable number of British style WCs, washbasins and hot showers in cubicles. We also assume that there will be an identified chemical toilet disposal point, and that the campsite will provide water and waste water drainage points and bin areas. If not the case, we comment. We do mention certain features that some readers find important: washbasins in cubicles, facilities for babies, facilities for those with disabilities and motorcaravan service points.

Reservations

Necessary for high season (roughly mid-July to mid-August) in popular holiday areas (i.e. beach resorts). You can reserve many sites via our own Alan Rogers Travel Service or through other tour operators. Remember, many sites are closed all winter and you may struggle to get an answer.

Telephone numbers

All numbers assume that you are phoning from within the country in question. From the UK or Ireland, dial 00, then the country's prefix (e.g. France is 33), then the campsite number given, but dropping the first '0'.

Opening dates

Dates given are those provided to us and can alter before the start of the season. If you intend to visit shortly after a published opening date, or shortly before the closing date, it is wise to check that it will actually be open at the time required. Similarly some sites operate a restricted service during the low season, only opening some of their facilities (e.g. swimming pools) during the main season; where we know about this, and have the relevant dates, we indicate it; again if you are at all doubtful it is wise to check.

Accommodation

Over recent years, more and more campsites have added high quality mobile homes, chalets, lodges, gites and more. Where applicable we indicate what is available and you'll find details online.

Special Offers

Some campsites have taken the opportunity to highlight a special offer. This is arranged by them and for clarification please contact the campsite direct.

What is **nature...?**

Nature means different things to different people. When camping (in any of its forms) it might mean a stunning, unspoilt setting; it might mean an absence of unnecessary facilities and a campsite stripped of technology. Others might prefer to drink in the exhilarating views, savour new experiences and still be able to check emails!

How do you camp?

With over 30,000 campsites in Europe, there are campsites in all kinds of natural environments. (Not to mention some – not featured in this guide – which have nothing natural about them at all).

Woodland camping

Camping among trees, or in clearings, always brings a very special atmosphere. The broadleaf forests of England conjure sentiments somewhere between Robin Hood and Squirrel Nutkin. The scented pine forests of Aquitaine have a definite 'Frenchness' about them, while the Bavarian forests evoke all kinds of Hansel and Gretel memories. When camping under a tree canopy you'll feel up close and personal with nature.

Coastal camping

The salty, fresh air of the seaside and drifting dunes or muddy estuaries always convey a natural, cleansing purity. Campsites might be right on the beach or set inland slightly but there are always plenty of educational activities for children.

Waterside camping

Campsites adjacent to rivers and lakes have their own natural charm. Shady banks, shallow margins, tumbling rapids all create a unique environment for unique wildlife and a unique playground for adults and children alike.

Mountain camping

Of course you don't have to be on some icy windswept peak in order to experience the glorious vistas, the clear air, the stillness and unique flora and fauna that come with camping at height. From England's craggy Peak District, to the Pyrenees, via the Alps to Scandinavian peaks and Italian Dolomites and beyond....

Rural camping

Those campsites based on a farm or amidst an agricultural landscape appeal to those who enjoy the feeling of space and freedom to roam that comes from big skies, rolling countryside and distant horizons.

Officially,
natural

The now well understood problem of recognising areas of outstanding natural beauty and interest, encouraging visitors to visit them, and then managing the impact caused by large numbers of visitors is largely managed by Europe's National Parks. Well over 350 of them in fact and between them featuring a huge range of landscape, from alpine to forest, from lakeland to grassland, from steppe to tidal basin.

The Europarc Federation brings together Europe's protected areas, unifying national parks, regional parks, nature parks and eco reserves in nearly 40 countries. The PAN Parks organisation represents some of the most important wilderness areas, developing sustainable tourism while protecting fragile regions.

The National Parks of Europe – **an overview**

- The Netherlands' 20 national parks include Hooge Veluwe Natural Park, the largest, whose forests, shifting sand dunes and heather-clad moors protect roe deer, boar and numerous species of birds.

- Ireland's 6 national parks, include Killarney National Park, in County Kerry, famed for its lake-studded mountains, and Connemara National Park with its lunar landscape of peat bogs.

- The UK's 14 national parks range from the wilds of Exmoor to the 16 lakes of the Lake District. Wales' Brecon Beacons, Pembrokeshire Coast and Snowdonia are truly dramatic, as are Scotland's parks of the Cairngorms and Loch Lomond.

- Germany's 14 national parks vary from the high mountains of Berchtesgaden to the beech forests of Eifel.

- Austria's 7 national parks cover 900 square miles of alpine massifs, forests and steppes.

- France's 7 national parks are all uniquely dramatic landscapes, including world-class sites in the Alps, Cévennes and the Pyrenees.

- Hungary's 10 parks include the famous Balaton High Country National Park.

- Sweden has 29 parks, all with huge mountains rising from glacial lakes, rivers and marshes and vast beech forests.

- Norway's 25 parks include lofty peaks, glaciers, evergreen forests and lakes.

- Spain's 13 parks, such as Picos de Europa and Ordesa in the Pyrenees, are a last refuge for endangered species.

- Portugal has 13 parks, including the home of the Iberian wolf and the royal eagle.

- Italy's 23 parks range from the mountainous Val d'Aoste, the Italian Alps and Pollino National Park, home to wolves and 40 metre tall pines, to Abruzzo with its endangered bears, chamois and wolves. Vesuvius National Park needs little introduction.

in **nature**

Being 'out there', immersed in nature, provides scope for all kinds of activities. It may take a while to shed the day-to-day habits and routines of daily life but an impromptu kite flying session, or an exploratory ramble along an enticing path can soon get you in the swing.

Two legs good, two wheels good

Walking and hiking are ever popular activities, being environmentally friendly and convenient. Cycle hire is often available (handy for collecting bread as well as exploring some beauty spots) and many campsites endeavour to make the most of their surroundings with marked trails. Indeed some of France's famous long distance paths (grandes randonnées) pass beside or even through some French campsites.

Children **and nature**

Children and nature go, well, hand in hand. Most youngsters are intrigued by bugs and mini beasts and something vaguely educational is also great fun and simple entertainment. The old favourite, Guessing the Petals, is always a winner: excellent for quiet concentration and awareness of nature, the aim is simply to guess the number of petals on a selection of flowers.

With nature trails, unusual birdlife, butterflies, squirrels, equestrian trails, perhaps rockpools, there's always something to engage, fascinate and teach. And of course, doing nothing has its own rewards too: when with young children try and do the unusual: take a short stroll, stop and stand for five minutes, listening and watching. You'll be amazed at what you observe together.

A natural **approach**

A number of campsite chains or marketing groups deliberately set out their stall to attract nature-lovers. Whereas some campsites have embraced the latest developments in infrastructure, groups like Sites et Paysages and Flower Camping have eschewed massive aqua parks in favour of enhancing their environmental and natural settings. Huttopia, working with the French Forestry Commission, offers a progressive style of camping which is actually 'retro' in its principles: think environmental commitment, small uncommercialised campsites with large 120m^2 pitches and a relaxed feel.
The Camping and Caravanning Club, with their Forest Holidays, offer woodland holidays with real eco-ethics. And some like Kawan Villages have integrated 'nature' activities into their on-site programmes, and worked hard on developing walking and cycling routes.

A natural
balance

For many ecologically minded campsites 'low impact' is a mantra. The environmental schemes like Bellamy and Clef Verte are just part of the bigger picture: the cycle of the seasons, the inter-reliance between plant and insect, predator and prey, crops and birdlife, fruit and wildlife, forest canopy and the eco-system of the woodland floor below. All this is important in maintaining natural balance and a thriving habitat. And campsites, being a vital link in a local community, form part of an unbroken chain too. Well managed campsites will value this, hence their emphasis on slow food, reduced food miles, locally produced artisan goods and the like.

Enjoy...!

Whether you're an 'old hand' or are contemplating your first trip, a regular reader of our Guides or a new 'convert', we wish you well in your travels and hope we have been able to help in some way. We are, of course, also out and about ourselves, visiting sites, talking to owners and readers, and generally checking on standards and new developments. We hope to bump into you!

Wishing you thoroughly enjoyable camping and caravanning in 2012 – favoured by good weather of course!

The Alan Rogers Team

Camping Picos de Europa

E-33556 Avín-Onís (Asturias)
t: 985 844 070   e: info@picos-europa.com
alanrogers.com/ES89650   www.picos-europa.com

Accommodation: ☑ Pitch ☑ Mobile home/chalet ☐ Hotel/B&B ☐ Apartment

This delightful site is, as its name suggests, an ideal spot from which to explore these dramatic limestone mountains on foot, by bicycle or on horseback. The site itself is continuously developing and the dynamic owner, José, and his nephew who helps out when he is away, are both very pleasant and nothing is too much trouble. The site is in a valley beside a pleasant, fast flowing river. The 160 marked pitches are of varying sizes and have been developed in three avenues, on level grass mostly backing on to hedging, with 6A electricity. An area for tents and apartments is over a bridge past the fairly small, but pleasant, round swimming pool. Local stone has been used for the L-shaped building at the main entrance which houses reception and a very good bar/restaurant. The site can organise caving activities, and has information about the Cares gorge along with the many energetic ways of exploring the area, including by canoe and quad-bike! The Bulnes funicular railway is well worth a visit.

You might like to know

Potholing is available – why not try this amazing underground experience accompanied by one of the campsite staff?

- ☐ Environmental accreditation
- ☑ Reduced energy/water consumption policy
- ☑ Recycling and reusing policy
- ☑ Information about walking and cycling
- ☑ Footpaths within 500 m. of the site
- ☑ Fishing within 1 km.
- ☐ Riding or pony trekking within 1 km.
- ☐ Direct river or lake access
- ☐ Within 10 km. of an area of outstanding natural beauty or national park
- ☑ Wildlife haven (on site/within 1 km)
- ☐ Public transport
- ☐ Dogs welcome

Facilities: Toilet facilities include a new fully equipped block, along with new facilities for disabled visitors and babies. Pleasant room with tables and chairs for poor weather. Washing machine and dryer. Shop (July-Sept). Swimming pool (Feb-Sept). Bar and cafeteria style restaurant (all year) serves a good value 'menu del dia' and snacks. WiFi in restaurant area. Play area. Fishing. Torches necessary in the new tent area. Off site: Riding 12 km. Bicycle hire 15 km. Golf and coast at Llanes 25 km.

Open: All year.

Directions: Avín is 15 km. east of Cangas de Onís on AS114 road to Panes and is probably best approached from this direction especially if towing. From A8 (Santander - Oviedo) use km. 326 exit and N634 northwest to Arriondas. Turn southeast on N625 to Cangas and join AS114 (Covodonga/Panes) by-passing Cangas. Site is just beyond Avín after 16 km. marker.
GPS: 43.3363, -4.94498

Charges guide

Per person	€ 5,02
child (under 14 yrs)	€ 4,01
pitch incl. car	€ 8,57 - € 9,64
electricity	€ 3,75

Camping Peña Montañesa

Ctra Ainsa - Francia km 2, E-22360 Labuerda (Huesca)
t: 974 500 032 e: info@penamontanesa.com
alanrogers.com/ES90600 www.penamontanesa.com

Accommodation: ☑ Pitch ☑ Mobile home/chalet ☐ Hotel/B&B ☐ Apartment

A large site situated quite high up in the Pyrenees near the Ordesa National Park, Peña Montañesa is easily accessible from Ainsa or from France via the Bielsa Tunnel (steep sections on the French side). The site is essentially divided into three sections opening progressively throughout the season and all have shade. The 288 pitches on fairly level grass are of about 75 sq.m. and 10A electricity is available on virtually all. Grouped near the entrance are the facilities that make the site so attractive, including a fair sized outdoor pool and a glass-covered indoor pool with jacuzzi and sauna. Here too is an attractive bar/restaurant with an open fire and a terrace, a supermarket and takeaway are opposite. There is an entertainment programme for children (21/6-15/9 and Easter weekend) and twice weekly for adults in July and August. This is quite a large site which has grown very quickly and as such, it may at times be a little hard pressed, although it is very well run. The site is ideally situated for exploring the beautiful Pyrenees.

You might like to know

Quad bikes can be hired locally and are a unique and fun way to explore the beautiful local countryside.

☐ Environmental accreditation
☐ Reduced energy/water consumption policy
☑ Recycling and reusing policy
☑ Information about walking and cycling
☑ Footpaths within 500 m. of the site
☐ Fishing within 1 km.
☐ Riding or pony trekking within 1 km.
☐ Direct river or lake access
☑ Within 10 km. of an area of outstanding natural beauty or national park
☑ Wildlife haven (on site/within 1 km)
☐ Public transport
☑ Dogs welcome

Facilities: A newer toilet block, heated when necessary, has free hot showers but cold water to open plan washbasins. Facilities for disabled visitors. Small baby room. An older block in the original area has similar provision. Washing machine and dryer. Bar, restaurant, takeaway and supermarket (all 1/1-31/12). Outdoor swimming pool (1/4-31/10). Indoor pool (all year). Playground. Boules. Bicycle hire. Riding. Rafting. Only gas barbecues are permitted. Torches required in some areas. Off site: Fishing 100 m. Skiing in season. Canoeing nearby.

Open: All year.

Directions: Site is 2 km. from Ainsa, on the road from Ainsa to France. GPS: 42.4352, 0.13618

Charges guide

Per unit incl. 2 persons and electricity	€ 24,60 - € 33,30

Camping Boltaña

Ctra N260 km 442, E-22340 Boltaña (Huesca)
t: 974 502 347 e: info@campingboltana.com
alanrogers.com/ES90620 www.campingboltana.com

Accommodation: ☑Pitch ☑Mobile home/chalet ☐ Hotel/B&B ☐ Apartment

Nestled in the Rio Ara valley, surrounded by the Pyrenees mountains and below a tiny but enchanting, historic, hill top village, is the very pretty, thoughtfully planned Camping Boltaña. Generously sized, 190 grassy pitches (all with 10A electricity) have good shade from a variety of trees and a stream meanders through the campsite. The landscaping includes ten charming rocky water gardens and a covered pergola doubles as an eating and play area. A stone building houses the site's reception, social room and supermarket. Angel Moreno, the owner of the site, is a charming host and has tried to think of everything to make his guests comfortable.

You might like to know

The campsite and its partner offer visitors the opportunity to try 'Hydrospeed', the latest extreme sport – swim into the rapids with just a board and flippers.

☐ Environmental accreditation
☑ Reduced energy/water consumption policy
☑ Recycling and reusing policy
☑ Information about walking and cycling
☑ Footpaths within 500 m. of the site
☐ Fishing within 1 km.
☐ Riding or pony trekking within 1 km.
☐ Direct river or lake access
☑ Within 10 km. of an area of outstanding natural beauty or national park
☑ Wildlife haven (on site/within 1 km)
☐ Public transport
☐ Dogs welcome

Facilities: Two modern sanitary blocks include facilities for disabled visitors and laundry facilities. Supermarket. Bar, restaurant and takeaway (1/7-31/8). Swimming pools (1/6-15/9). Playground. Barbecues. Entertainment for children (high season). Pétanque. Guided tours, plus hiking, canyoning, rafting, climbing, mountain biking and caving. Torches useful in some parts. Off site: Local bus service.

Open: 15 January - 15 December.

Directions: South of the Park Nacional de Ordesa, site is about 50 km. from Jaca near Ainsa. From Ainsa travel northwest on N260 toward Boltaña (near 443 km. marker) and 1 km. from Boltaña turn south toward Margudgued. Site is well signed and is 1 km. along this road. GPS: 42.43018, 0.07882

Charges guide

Per unit incl. 2 persons and electricity	€ 35,40
extra person	€ 6,50
child (1-10 yrs)	€ 5,50
dog	€ 3,25

Camping La Fresneda

Partida Vall del Pi, E-44596 La Fresneda (Teruel)
t: 978 854 085 e: info@campinglafresneda.com
alanrogers.com/ES91100 www.campinglafresneda.com

Accommodation: ☑ Pitch ☐ Mobile home/chalet ☐ Hotel/B&B ☐ Apartment

La Fresneda is a great little campsite, situated on three terraces at the foot of a wooded escarpment and overlooking the huge valley of the National Reserve of Los Puertos de Beceite. Everything is in line with the natural beauty of the area and the very clean, very well equipped, toilet block is partly underground. There are 25 pitches with grass and gravel surfaces, all used for touring and with 6A electricity. The site is quite new and the enthusiastic Dutch owners, Jet Knijn and her partner Joost Leeuwenberg, built it from scratch, recently adding a shady garden atrium with a terrace and plunge pool for guests to relax and enjoy the views. The cosy bar is in rustic style with a terrace to enjoy your afternoon drink whilst enjoying a view of the valley. The adjacent small town of La Fresneda is situated on the top of a hill and is part of the Spanish National Heritage. There are many routes for walking and cycling in the National Reserve Los Puertos de Beceite as well as directly from the campsite.

You might like to know

A particular attraction of the site is its close proximity to a number of fascinating museums, including the Picasso Museum, the Olive Oil Museum and the Paleonotology Museum.

☐ Environmental accreditation
☐ Reduced energy/water consumption policy
☑ Recycling and reusing policy
☑ Information about walking and cycling
☑ Footpaths within 500 m. of the site
☐ Fishing within 1 km.
☐ Riding or pony trekking within 1 km.
☐ Direct river or lake access
☐ Within 10 km. of an area of outstanding natural beauty or national park
☑ Wildlife haven (on site/within 1 km)
☐ Public transport
☐ Dogs welcome

Facilities: Toilet block with hot water throughout. Washing machine. Bar with terrace where meals are served a few times a week. Fresh bread daily. Garden atrium with terrace and plunge pool. Bicycle hire. Information on walking and cycling routes. Gas barbecue for hire. Pets are not accepted. Off site: Baker, grocer and butcher in the village. Supermarkets at Alcañiz 30 minutes drive. Riding 10 km. Fishing 20 km. A 'Green Track' is nearby, an almost flat cycle way which was once a railway. Small Picasso museum at Horta de San Joan.

Open: 1 April - 1 October.

Directions: From the N232 (Alcañiz - Vinaros, Castellón) turn off just east of Valdealgorfa (at Restaurant Las Ventas) onto A231 to Valjunquera/Valderrobres, then La Fresneda. GPS: 40.90695, 0.061667

Charges guide

Per person	€ 5,00
child (0-1 yrs)	free
pitch incl. electricity	€ 12,00

PORTUGAL – Campo do Gerês

Parque de Campismo de Cerdeira

Rua de Cerdeira 400, P-4840 Campo do Gerês (Braga)
t: 253 351 005 e: info@parquecerdeira.com
alanrogers.com/PO8370 www.parquecerdeira.com

Accommodation: ☑Pitch ☑Mobile home/chalet ☐ Hotel/B&B ☐ Apartment

Located in the national park of Peneda Gerês, amidst spectacular mountain scenery, this excellent site offers modern facilities in a truly natural area. The national park is home to all manner of flora, fauna and wildlife, including the roebuck, wolf and wild boar. The well fenced, professional and peaceful site has some 600 good sized, unmarked, mostly level, grassy pitches in a shady woodland setting. Electricity is available for most pitches, though some long leads may be required. A very large timber complex, tastefully designed with the use of noble materials, granite and wood, provides a superb restaurant with a comprehensive menu. A pool with a separated section for toddlers is a welcome, cooling relief in the height of summer. There are unlimited opportunities in the immediate area for fishing, riding, canoeing, mountain biking and climbing, so take advantage of this quality mountain hospitality.

You might like to know

Nature lovers will be in their element in the Peneda-Gerês National Park, a haven for wildlife including the wolf and royal eagle. Human occupation dates back 7,000 years and ancient artefacts are frequently unearthed.

- ☑ Environmental accreditation
- ☑ Reduced energy/water consumption policy
- ☑ Recycling and reusing policy
- ☑ Information about walking and cycling
- ☐ Footpaths within 500 m. of the site
- ☑ Fishing within 1 km.
- ☑ Riding or pony trekking within 1 km.
- ☐ Direct river or lake access
- ☐ Within 10 km. of an area of outstanding natural beauty or national park
- ☑ Wildlife haven (on site/within 1 km)
- ☐ Public transport
- ☐ Dogs welcome

Facilities: Four very clean sanitary blocks provide mixed style WCs, controllable showers and hot water. Laundry. Gas supplies. Shop. Restaurant/bar (1/4- 6/10, plus weekends and holidays). Playground. Bicycle hire. TV room (satellite). Medical post. Good tennis courts. Minigolf. Car wash. Barbecue area. Torches useful. English spoken. Attractive bungalows to rent. Dogs are not accepted June-Aug. Off site: Fishing and riding 800 m.

Open: All year.

Directions: From north, N103 (Braga - Chaves), turn left at N205 (7.5 km. north of Braga). Follow N205 to Caldelas Terras de Bouro and Covide where site is clearly marked to Campo do Geres. An eastern approach from the N103 is for the adventurous but will be rewarded by magnificent views over mountains and lakes.
GPS: 41.7631, -8.1905

Charges guide

Per unit incl. 2 persons and electricity	€ 15,75 - € 24,45
extra person	€ 3,20 - € 4,60
child (5-11 yrs)	€ 2,00 - € 3,10
dog	€ 1,50 - € 3,00

Dolomiti Camping Village

Via Gole 105, I-38025 Dimaro (Trentino - Alto Adige)
t: 0463 974 332 e: info@campingdolomiti.com
alanrogers.com/IT61830 www.campingdolomiti.com

Accommodation: ☑Pitch ☑Mobile home/chalet ☐ Hotel/B&B ☐ Apartment

Dolomiti di Brenta is open for separate winter and summer seasons. It is situated at an altitude of 800 m. in an attractive open valley surrounded by the rugged Dolomite Mountains, and is only 100 m. from the River Noce. It is an ideal base to explore this fantastic region. There are 195 level and grassy pitches, all with 4A electricity and some fully serviced. Young trees offer a little shade. The pitches range in size from small (45 sq. m), suitable for small tents, to large (100 sq.m) suitable for medium sized outfits. The Dolomites are one of the most spectacular unspoilt mountain regions of Europe and it is easy to go off the beaten track and find some real peace and quiet. It is close to the Estelvio national park, the largest in Italy and home to a wide variety of flora and fauna. The area can be explored on foot, by mountain bike or in the car, and energetic families can enjoy a wide range of activities on the river or in the surrounding mountains.

Special offers
Two night camping stay includes spa entrance, 30 minute massage, pool and outdoor sports: € 155/pers.

You might like to know
The campsite is located between two different national parks and within easy reach of the Brenta Dolomites, ideal for trekking, mountain biking, rafting and skiing.

- ☑ Environmental accreditation
- ☑ Reduced energy/water consumption policy
- ☑ Recycling and reusing policy
- ☑ Information about walking and cycling
- ☑ Footpaths within 500 m. of the site
- ☑ Fishing within 1 km.
- ☐ Riding or pony trekking within 1 km.
- ☑ Direct river or lake access
- ☑ Within 10 km. of an area of outstanding natural beauty or national park
- ☐ Wildlife haven (on site/within 1 km)
- ☑ Public transport
- ☑ Dogs welcome

Facilities: Modern toilet block with all necessary facilities including private bathrooms for rent. Washing machine, dryer. Small shop. Bar, restaurant, pizzeria. Outdoor swimming pool and spa. Fitness centre. Large children's play area. Communal barbecues. Football. Volleyball. WiFi. Off site: Attractive mountain villages with their local craft shops and the Estelvio national park. Many marked hiking and biking trails. Shops, bars, restaurant and pool in Malè.

Open: 4 December - 10 April and 21 May - 25 September.

Directions: Leave the A22, Brenner motorway at San Michele All'Adige, about 40 km. south of Bolzano. Follow signs for SS43 through Cles, then SS42 through Malè. 19 km. after Cles turn left in Via Gole, site is on right. GPS: 46.325278, 10.863056

Charges guide

Per unit incl. 2 persons and electricity	€ 26,40 - € 42,70
dog (not July/Aug)	€ 3,00 - € 4,00

Camping Arquin

Feldgatterweg 25, I-39011 Lana (Trentino - Alto Adige)
t: 0473 561 187 e: info@camping-arquin.com
alanrogers.com/IT61865 www.camping-arquin.it

Accommodation: ☑Pitch ☑Mobile home/chalet ☐ Hotel/B&B ☐ Apartment

Camping Arquin is in the South Tirol (Alto Adige) where the majority of the population speak German. It is open from early March to mid November and lies in an open valley surrounded by orchards, beyond which are high mountains. This is a region of natural beauty and is famous for its flowery meadows. The site is close to the village of Lana, one of the largest in the South Tyrol and famous for its Mediterranean climate. There are 120 small, sunny, level, grass pitches all with 6A electricity and many are fully serviced. There is a wide range of marked footpaths and cycling routes. This is a good base for active families wishing to explore the local area on foot, by bicycle, in the car, by bus or by train. The higher reaches of the mountains can be accessed by cable car. This area is also known for its thermal springs and baths. The interesting old town of Meran is only 7 km. and is accessible by bus.

You might like to know

Whatever the season, there is plenty to enjoy – swimming in summer and hiking during autumn, all in a beautiful natural landscape.

☐ Environmental accreditation
☐ Reduced energy/water consumption policy
☑ Recycling and reusing policy
☑ Information about walking and cycling
☐ Footpaths within 500 m. of the site
☐ Fishing within 1 km.
☐ Riding or pony trekking within 1 km.
☐ Direct river or lake access
☐ Within 10 km. of an area of outstanding natural beauty or national park
☐ Wildlife haven (on site/within 1 km)
☑ Public transport
☑ Dogs welcome

Facilities: Modern toilet block with all necessary facilities including those for babies and disabled visitors. Motorcaravan services. Small shop. Restaurant and bar. Small swimming pool. Children's play area. Internet point. Off site: Bus stop 200 m. Large swimming pool 200 m. (May onwards; free to campers). Historical town of Meran 7 km. Museums. Golf. Biking. Hiking. Tennis. Paragliding. Rock climbing. Canoeing. Nature parks. Cable car.

Open: 1 March - 15 November.

Directions: Leave A22, Brenner Motorway at Bozen Süd. Take Expressway towards Meran. At the exit Lana-Burgstall turn left. After 250 m. take first right, follow signs to site. GPS: 46.611151, 11.174434

Charges guide

Per unit incl. 2 persons and electricity	€ 30,00 - € 34,00
dog	free

Caravan Park Sexten

Saint Josef Strasse 54, I-39030 Sexten (Trentino - Alto Adige)
t: 047 471 0444 e: info@caravanparksexten.it
alanrogers.com/IT62030 www.caravanparksexten.it

Accommodation: ☑Pitch ☑Mobile home/chalet ☐ Hotel/B&B ☐ Apartment

Caravan Park Sexten is 1,520 metres above sea level and has 268 pitches, some very large and all with electricity (16A), TV connections and water and drainage in summer and winter (underground heating stops pipes freezing). Some pitches are in the open to catch the sun, others are tucked in forest clearings by the river. They are mostly gravelled to provide an ideal all-year surface. It is the facilities that make this a truly remarkable site; no expense or effort has been spared to create a luxurious environment that matches that of any top class hotel. The health spa has every type of sauna, Turkish and Roman baths, sunbeds, herbal and hay baths, hairdressing and beauty treatment salons, relaxation and massage rooms and a remarkable indoor pool with children's pool, Kneipp therapy pool and whirlpools. The timber of the buildings is from 400-year-old farmhouses, used with modern materials to create amazing interiors and (mainly) authentic Tyrolean exteriors. A member of Leading Campings Group.

You might like to know

The campsite is located near one of the most beautiful and majestic of the Dolomites mountains.

- ☐ Environmental accreditation
- ☑ Reduced energy/water consumption policy
- ☑ Recycling and reusing policy
- ☑ Information about walking and cycling
- ☑ Footpaths within 500 m. of the site
- ☐ Fishing within 1 km.
- ☑ Riding or pony trekking within 1 km.
- ☐ Direct river or lake access
- ☑ Within 10 km. of an area of outstanding natural beauty or national park
- ☑ Wildlife haven (on site/within 1 km)
- ☑ Public transport
- ☑ Dogs welcome

Facilities: The three main toilet blocks are remarkable in design, fixtures and fittings. Heated floors. Controllable showers. Hairdryers. Luxurious private facilities to rent. Children and baby rooms. En-suite facilities for disabled visitors. Laundry facilities. Motorcaravan services. Shop. Bars and restaurants with entertainment 2-3 nights a week. Indoor pool. Heated outdoor pool (1/6-30/9). Health spa. New play area. Activities for all. Tennis. Bicycle hire. Climbing wall. Fishing. Adventure activity packages. Internet access. WiFi (whole site). Off site: Skiing in winter (free bus to 2 ski lifts within 5 km). Walking, cycling and climbing. Riding and golf.

Open: All year.

Directions: Sexten/Sesto is 110 km. northeast of Bolzano. From Bressanone/Brixen exit on the A22 Brenner-Modena motorway follow the SS49 east for about 60 km. Turn south on the SS52 at Innichen/San Candido and follow signs to Sexten. Site is 5 km. past village (signed). GPS: 46.66727, 12.40221

Charges guide

Per unit incl. 2 persons	€ 22,00 - € 49,00
extra person	€ 8,00 - € 13,00
child (2-14 yrs)	€ 4,50 - € 11,00
electricity per kWh (16A)	€ 0,70

Camping Seiser Alm

Saint Konstantin 16, I-39050 Völs am Schlern (Trentino - Alto Adige)
t: 047 170 6459 e: info@camping-seiseralm.com
alanrogers.com/IT62040 www.camping-seiseralm.com

Accommodation: ☑ Pitch ☑ Mobile home/chalet ☐ Hotel/B&B ☐ Apartment

What an amazing experience awaits you at Seiser Alm! Elisabeth and Erhard Mahlknecht have created a superb site in the magnificent Südtirol region of the Dolomite mountains. Towering peaks provide a magnificent backdrop when you dine in the charming, traditional style restaurant on the upper terrace. Here you will also find the bar, shop and reception. The 150 touring pitches are of a very high standard with 16A electricity supply, 120 with gas, water, drainage and satellite connections. Guests were delighted with the site when we visited, many coming to walk or cycle, some just to enjoy the surroundings. There are countless things to see and do here. Enjoy the grand 18-hole golf course alongside the site or join the organised excursions and activities. Local buses and cable cars provide an excellent service for summer visitors and skiers alike (discounts are available). In keeping with the natural setting, the majority of the luxury facilities are set into the hillside.

You might like to know

The site is adjacent to the Dolomites (a UNESCO world heritage site). The range numbers 18 peaks which rise to above 3,000 metres and cover 141,903 ha.

☑ Environmental accreditation
☑ Reduced energy/water consumption policy
☑ Recycling and reusing policy
☑ Information about walking and cycling
☐ Footpaths within 500 m. of the site
☑ Fishing within 1 km.
☐ Riding or pony trekking within 1 km.
☐ Direct river or lake access
☑ Within 10 km. of an area of outstanding natural beauty or national park
☑ Wildlife haven (on site/within 1 km)
☑ Public transport
☑ Dogs welcome

Facilities: One luxury underground block. 16 private units are available. Excellent facilities for disabled visitors and children. Underfloor heating. Constant fresh air ventilation. Washing machines and drying room. Sauna. Supermarket. Quality restaurant and bar with terrace. Entertainment programme. Miniclub. Children's adventure park and play room. Special rooms for ski equipment. Torches useful. WiFi (charged). Apartments and mobile homes for rent. Off site: Riding alongside site. 18-hole golf course and fishing 1 km. Bicycle hire and lake swimming 2 km. Skiing in winter.

Open: All year excl. 2 November - 20 December.

Directions: From A22-E45 take Bolzano Nord exit. Take road for Prato Isarco/Blumau, then road for Fie/Völs. Take care as the split in the road is sudden and if you miss the left fork as you enter a tunnel (Altopiano dello Sciliar/Schlerngebiet) you will pay a heavy price in extra kilometres. Enjoy the climb to Völs am Schlern. Site signed. GPS: 46.53344, 11.53335

Charges guide

Per unit incl. 2 persons	€ 17,30 - € 43,50
extra person	€ 6,90 - € 9,50
child (2-16 yrs)	€ 3,60 - € 7,70
electricity (per kWh)	€ 0,60

Camping Kiefernhain

Kiefernhain 37, I-39026 Prad am Stilfserjoch (Trentino - Alto Adige)
t: 047 361 6422 e: kiefernhain@rolmail.net
alanrogers.com/IT62060 www.camping-kiefernhain.it

Accommodation: ☑ Pitch ☐ Mobile home/chalet ☐ Hotel/B&B ☐ Apartment

The Stelvio National Park is arguably Italy's premier Alpine park. Camping Kiefernhain lies within the park in the Val Venosta. There are 180 touring pitches here – some well shaded, others with much sunnier settings. Many pitches have fine views across to the Otztaler Alps. All have 6A electrical connections. A public swimming pool is adjacent to the site with free access for campers. Other amenities are available in a nearby sports centre or in the village, five minutes away on foot.

You might like to know

This campsite is ideal for those looking for a quiet and relaxing holiday in a natural setting. The submerged village of Graun is still visible in the lake, where the bell tower rises from the water.

- ☑ Environmental accreditation
- ☑ Reduced energy/water consumption policy
- ☑ Recycling and reusing policy
- ☑ Information about walking and cycling
- ☐ Footpaths within 500 m. of the site
- ☑ Fishing within 1 km.
- ☐ Riding or pony trekking within 1 km.
- ☐ Direct river or lake access
- ☐ Within 10 km. of an area of outstanding natural beauty or national park
- ☑ Wildlife haven (on site/within 1 km)
- ☐ Public transport
- ☑ Dogs welcome

Facilities: Bar/café and small shop. Playground. Guided walking excursions. Motorcaravan services. Off site: Swimming pool (free access). Bus stop 100 m. Village centre 300 m. Golf. Walking and cycling trails, mountain biking.

Open: Easter - 3 October.

Directions: From the A22 autostrada take the Bozen (south) exit and join the S38 passing Merano and Silandro. At Spondigna head south (still on the S38) to the village of Prato allo Stelvio, from where the site is well signed. GPS: 46.62536, 10.59485

Charges guide

Per unit incl. 2 persons and electricity	€ 25,60 - € 36,60
extra person	€ 6,50 - € 10,50
child (2-15 yrs)	€ 4,50 - € 6,50
dog	€ 3,50 - € 4,00

ITALY – Predazzo

Camping Valle Verde

Loc. Ischia 2, Sotto Sassa, I-38037 Predazzo (Trentino - Alto Adige)
t: 046 250 2394 e: info@campingvalleverde.it
alanrogers.com/IT62105 www.campingvalleverde.it

Accommodation: ☑ Pitch ☑ Mobile home/chalet ☐ Hotel/B&B ☐ Apartment

Camping Valle Verde lies at an altitude of 1080 m. in a beautiful green valley surrounded by meadows, woods and mountain streams. It is only 2 km. from Predazzo and enjoys all the facilities of this well known mountain village. There are 122 average size, level, grass pitches, all with 3A electricity and some with a little shade. Access is good for large outfits. This area is ideal for lovers of nature; close by are crystal clear alpine lakes, woods and a wide variety of flora and fauna. Find time to relax and enjoy the rhythms of nature. For lovers of sports and the more adventurous, one can participate in hang-gliding, rafting and rock climbing. For the less adventurous there are many marked hiking and mountain bike trails starting close to the campsite. Predazzo, well known for its traditions, cultural heritage and hospitality, is both a summer and winter resort.

You might like to know

This family run campsite in the peaceful Dolomites countryside combines nature, sport and culture – perfect for a relaxing holiday.

☐ Environmental accreditation
☐ Reduced energy/water consumption policy
☑ Recycling and reusing policy
☑ Information about walking and cycling
☑ Footpaths within 500 m. of the site
☑ Fishing within 1 km.
☐ Riding or pony trekking within 1 km.
☑ Direct river or lake access
☑ Within 10 km. of an area of outstanding natural beauty or national park
☑ Wildlife haven (on site/within 1 km)
☐ Public transport
☑ Dogs welcome

Facilities: Modern toilet block with all necessary facilities including those for babies and campers with disabilities. Washing machine/dryer. Motorcaravan services. Restaurant with limited menu, snack bar, takeaway (mid May-mid Sept). Play area. Sports area. Volleyball. Football. Table tennis. Swimming in adjacent stream. Bicycle hire. WiFi (charged). Off site: Indoor pool, tennis, rock climbing, pony trekking, shops, bars and restaurants in Predazzo 2 km. Marked walks and cycle routes. Hang-gliding, Rafting.

Open: 1 May - 30 September.

Directions: Leave A22 Brenner motorway, south of Bolzano, signed Ora. From Ora take SS48 to Calvalese (20 km), then SS232 to Predazzo. Pass the Alpine School of Financial Police then first right signed Bellamonte and Paneveggio. After minigolf take first right to site. GPS: 46.310565, 11.631764

Charges guide

Per unit incl. 2 persons and electricity	€ 22,40 - € 28,80
dog	€ 2,00 - € 3,00

Camping Val Rendena

Via Civico 117, I-38080 Darè (Trentino - Alto Adige)
t: 046 580 1669 e: info@campingvalrendena.com
alanrogers.com/IT62135 www.campingvalrendena.com

Accommodation: ☑Pitch ☑Mobile home/chalet ☐Hotel/B&B ☑Apartment

Set in the National Park of Adamello Brenta, a refuge of the European brown bear, Camping Val Rendena, is an enthusiastically run family site with a very friendly feel. There are 52 level grass touring pitches with some tree shade, all with 6A electricity and spaced between the seasonal pitches. The site's location makes it an ideal base from which to explore this beautiful region, rich in flora and fauna, where wooded hills with many marked paths reach up to 1,800 m. Beside the site runs the Sarca River, bordered for much of its journey by a cycle way. The park has several interesting information centres, including one at Spormaggiore where brown bears can be observed. In the friendly reception a host of very useful park information is available informing visitors of what this region has to offer. At the top of the valley is the 1,500 m. high ski resort of Madonna di Campiglio where, below the tree line, forests of larch and pine shade the endless routes for walkers, mountain bike and cycle riders.

You might like to know

The village of Darè is located in Val Rendena, not far from the famous skiing areas of Pinzolo.

- ☐ Environmental accreditation
- ☐ Reduced energy/water consumption policy
- ☑ Recycling and reusing policy
- ☑ Information about walking and cycling
- ☑ Footpaths within 500 m. of the site
- ☐ Fishing within 1 km.
- ☐ Riding or pony trekking within 1 km.
- ☑ Direct river or lake access
- ☑ Within 10 km. of an area of outstanding natural beauty or national park
- ☑ Wildlife haven (on site/within 1 km)
- ☐ Public transport
- ☑ Dogs welcome

Facilities: Two sanitary units include free hot water, controllable showers, some washbasins in cabins. Facilities for disabled visitors. Baby room. Laundry. Motorcaravan services. Shop selling essentials. Solar heated swimming pool with adjoining children's pool (1/6-30/9). Large playing field. Play area and play room. Bicycle hire. Communal barbecue. Massage and other treatments by appointment. Eight apartments to rent. Off site: Pizza restaurant adjoins site. Thermal baths. Golf. Tennis.

Open: 10 May - 30 September.

Directions: From the A22 (E45) Brenner - Verona autostrada take exit for Trento-Centro. Then travel westerly on the SS45b to Sarche, then SS237 to Ponte Arche and Tione di Trento. From here head north on the SS239 (Madonna di Campiglio) for about 10 km. to Darè. Immediately after entering Darè take descending slip road to the right then follow signs to site beside river. Do not follow GPS instructions to enter small lane to right before Darè as this leads to a narrow, height restricted bridge. GPS: 46.07440, 10.71718

Charges guide

Per unit incl. 2 persons and electricity	€ 24,60 - € 28,60
extra person	€ 7,80 - € 8,80
child (3-12 yrs)	€ 6,80 - € 7,80

Camping Villaggio dei Fiori

Via Tiro a Volo 3, I-18038 San Remo (Ligúria)
t: 018 466 0635   e: info@villaggiodeifiori.it
alanrogers.com/IT64010   www.villaggiodeifiori.it

Accommodation: ☑ Pitch ☑ Mobile home/chalet ☐ Hotel/B&B ☐ Apartment

Open all year round, this open and spacious site has high standards and is ideal for exploring the Italian Riviera or for just relaxing by the enjoyable, filtered sea water pools. Unusually all the pitch areas at the site are totally paved and there are some extremely large pitches for large units (ask reception to open another gate for entry). All 200 pitches have electricity (3/6A), 50 also have water and drainage, and there is an outside sink and cold water for every four. There is ample shade from mature trees and shrubs, which are constantly watered and cared for in summer. The 'gold' pitches and some wonderful tent pitches are along the seafront with great views. There is a path to a secluded and pleasant beach with sparkling waters, overlooked by a large patio area. The rocky surrounds are excellent for snorkelling and fishing, with ladder access to the water. The friendly management speak excellent English and will supply detailed touring plans. Activities and entertainment are organised in high season for adults and children.

You might like to know

Every year, there is lots going on close to the campsite, including the nostalgic Sanremo Veteran Car Rally with its special event for former stars of the racing world.

☑ Environmental accreditation
☑ Reduced energy/water consumption policy
☑ Recycling and reusing policy
☐ Information about walking and cycling
☐ Footpaths within 500 m. of the site
☐ Fishing within 1 km.
☐ Riding or pony trekking within 1 km.
☑ Direct river or lake access
☐ Within 10 km. of an area of outstanding natural beauty or national park
☐ Wildlife haven (on site/within 1 km)
☑ Public transport
☐ Dogs welcome

Facilities: Three clean and modern toilet blocks have British and Turkish style WCs and hot water throughout. Baby rooms. Facilities for disabled campers. Laundry facilities. Motorcaravan services. Bar sells essential supplies. Large restaurant. Pizzeria and takeaway (all year). Sea water swimming pools (small extra charge in high season) and heated whirlpool spa (June-Sept). Tennis. Excellent play area. Fishing. Satellite TV. Internet access. WiFi (free after 7 days hire). Bicycle hire. Gas delivered to pitch. Dogs are not accepted. Off site: Bus at gate. Supermarket 100 m. Shop 150 m. Riding and golf 2 km. 24 km. cycle route to the city.

Open: All year.

Directions: From SS1 (Ventimiglia - Imperia), site is on right just before San Remo. There is a sharp right turn if approaching from the west. From autostrada A10 take San Remo Ouest exit. Site is well signed. GPS: 43.80117, 7.74867

Charges guide

Per unit incl. 4 persons and electricity	€ 35,00 - € 72,00

Camping La Verna

Localitá Vezzano, I-52010 Chiusi della Verna (Tuscany)
t: 057 553 2121 e: info@campinglaverna.it
alanrogers.com/IT66130 www.campinglaverna.it

Accommodation: ☑ Pitch ☐ Mobile home/chalet ☐ Hotel/B&B ☐ Apartment

Camping La Verna is a rustic campsite, 850 m. above sea level, on the edge of the Casentino National Forest and close to the beautiful historic village of Chiusi della Verna, which is widely known as an area of religious retreat and pilgrimage. Camping La Verna has basic facilities including a small pool, a bar and a restaurant/pizzeria. The shaded pitches of varying sizes are on terraces dotted throughout tall trees. Mostly level, all have 10A electricity and are on grass and sand. This is a peaceful and remote site suitable for campers who enjoy simple pleasures. There are medieval hamlets and other sites of interest in the area, including the sanctuary of San Francesco. This village is known for its association with Francis of Assisi and as the birthplace of Michelangelo whose father was governor of the area. Della la Chiusi is near the ancient Via Major, an important Roman road making the area an ancient centre of commercial enterprise.

You might like to know

There's something of interest for everyone – castles, monasteries and churches, and some lovely old towns such as Bibbiena, Capolona and Poppi.

- ☐ Environmental accreditation
- ☐ Reduced energy/water consumption policy
- ☑ Recycling and reusing policy
- ☑ Information about walking and cycling
- ☑ Footpaths within 500 m. of the site
- ☐ Fishing within 1 km.
- ☐ Riding or pony trekking within 1 km.
- ☐ Direct river or lake access
- ☑ Within 10 km. of an area of outstanding natural beauty or national park
- ☑ Wildlife haven (on site/within 1 km)
- ☑ Public transport
- ☑ Dogs welcome

Facilities: One dated toilet block includes mixed Turkish and British style WCs and push-button showers. No facilities for disabled visitors. Washing machines. Bar, restaurant and pizzeria with small terrace. Communal barbecues only. Torches very useful. Off site: Riding and ATM 1 km. Exploration of the world-famous religious and commercial centre.

Open: Easter - October.

Directions: Site is in village of Chiusi della Verna, north of Arezzo. From E45 (south or north) go to Pieve Sto Stefano. From here take P208 to Chiusi della Verna. Site is well signed in the village. Approaching from the west on the P208 be prepared for a very long winding drive (great views but hard driving). GPS: 43.69780, 11.92351

Charges guide

Per person	€ 5,50 - € 7,00
child (3-10 yrs)	€ 4,00 - € 5,50
pitch incl. electricity	€ 6,50 - € 8,50

Camping Il Collaccio

I-06047 Castelvecchio di Preci (Umbria)
t: 074 393 9005 e: info@ilcollaccio.com
alanrogers.com/IT66560 www.ilcollaccio.com

Accommodation: ☑Pitch ☑Mobile home/chalet ☐ Hotel/B&B ☐ Apartment

Castelvecchio di Preci is tucked away in the tranquil depths of the Umbrian countryside. The natural beauty of the Monti Sibillini National Park is nearby (excursions are organised) and there are walking and cycling opportunities with many marked paths. The camping area here has been carved out of the hillside and forms a natural amphitheatre with splendid views. At first sight the narrow, steep entrance seems daunting (the owner will assist) and the road leading down to the rather steep camping terraces takes one to the exit. The 114 large pitches are on level terraces with stunning views. Electricity (6A) is available – long leads useful. Il Collaccio is owned and run by the Baldoni family who bought the farm over 30 years ago, rebuilt the derelict farmhouse in its original style and then decided to share it with holiday-makers. The farming aspect was kept, together with a unit producing salami and its products can be bought in the shop and sampled in the excellent restaurant. Small tour operator presence.

You might like to know

Relax and enjoy the beautiful views, from the swimming pool or from the restaurant terrace.

☐ Environmental accreditation
☑ Reduced energy/water consumption policy
☑ Recycling and reusing policy
☑ Information about walking and cycling
☐ Footpaths within 500 m. of the site
☐ Fishing within 1 km.
☐ Riding or pony trekking within 1 km.
☐ Direct river or lake access
☐ Within 10 km. of an area of outstanding natural beauty or national park
☑ Wildlife haven (on site/within 1 km)
☐ Public transport
☑ Dogs welcome

Facilities: Three modern sanitary blocks spaced through the site have British and Turkish style WCs, cold water in washbasins and hot, pre-mixed water in showers and sinks. Facilities for disabled visitors. Washing machine. Motorcaravan services. Bar, restaurant and takeaway. Shop (basics, 1/6-20/9). Two swimming pools (20/5-30/9). Play area. Tennis. Boules. Entertainment in high season. Excursions. Off site: Cycling and walking. Canoeing and rafting 2 km. Fishing 10 km.

Open: 1 April - 30 September.

Directions: From SS77 Foligno-Civitonova Marche road turn south at Muccia for Visso from where Preci is signed. There is a direct route through a new tunnel, if the site is approached north of Eggi which is 10 km. north of Spoleto. The tunnel exit is at Sant Anatolia di Narco SS209, where a left turn is to Preci.
GPS: 42.888, 13.01464

Charges guide

Per person	€ 6,00 - € 9,50
child (3-12 yrs)	€ 3,00 - € 6,00
caravan and car	€ 10,00 - € 16,00
motorcaravan	€ 8,50 - € 13,00
tent	€ 6,00 - € 9,50

Camping Baia di Gallipoli

Litoranea per Santa Maria di Leuca, I-73014 Gallipoli (Puglia)
t: 083 327 3210 e: info@baiadigallipoli.com
alanrogers.com/IT68660 www.baiadigallipoli.com

Accommodation: ☑Pitch ☑Mobile home/chalet ☐ Hotel/B&B ☐ Apartment

The western shoreline of Puglia offers beaches of excellent quality, interspersed with small villages and some holiday complexes. The Baia di Gallipoli campsite is in a quiet rural area to the southwest of the town on a minor coast road. It offers 600 pitches, all with electricity, under pine and eucalyptus trees. Cars are parked in a separate area and access for vehicles is strictly controlled which gives the site a quiet, peaceful ambience. Although it is about 1 km. from the beach it has solved that problem in partnership with others by providing regular shuttle buses to the beach car park. The sites jointly fund a bar and restaurant on the beach with toilets and showers. The short walk to the beach from the car park is along a timber walk and site staff clear the beach and the pine wood behind of rubbish daily. Michele Annese and the other staff clearly have a pride in their work and this is reflected in the standards offered and maintained. This is a good, quiet site in low season and also great for family holidays in July and August.

You might like to know
Very close to the beach (800 m) and surrounded by old olive trees, this campsite has a typical mediterranean atmosphere.

☐ Environmental accreditation
☐ Reduced energy/water consumption policy
☑ Recycling and reusing policy
☑ Information about walking and cycling
☐ Footpaths within 500 m. of the site
☐ Fishing within 1 km.
☐ Riding or pony trekking within 1 km.
☐ Direct river or lake access
☑ Within 10 km. of an area of outstanding natural beauty or national park
☑ Wildlife haven (on site/within 1 km)
☐ Public transport
☑ Dogs welcome

Facilities: Five toilet blocks include facilities for disabled visitors, both on the site and at the beach. Motorcaravan service point. Washing machines. Shop. Bar and restaurant (1/4-31/10). Swimming pool (1/6-30/9). Tennis. Shuttle bus to beach (1 km). Off site: Gallipoli.

Open: 1 April - 30 September.

Directions: The SS101 motorway south of Bari heads first to Lecce, then turns southwest towards Gallipoli. Join the SS274 towards Santa Maria di Leuca and exit at Lido Pizzo. Follow the coast road (SP215) towards Gallipoli and site is on the right 4 km. before Gallipoli. GPS: 39.998317, 18.0265

Charges guide

Per unit incl. 2 persons and electricity	€ 23,50 - € 48,00
extra person	€ 8,50 - € 13,50
child (3-8 yrs)	free - € 8,00
dog	€ 1,50 - € 3,00

Kamp Klin

Lepena 1, SLO-5232 Soca
t: 053 889 513 e: kampklin@siol.net
alanrogers.com/SV4235

Accommodation: ☑Pitch ☑Mobile home/chalet ☐ Hotel/B&B ☐ Apartment

With an attractive location surrounded by mountains in the Triglav National Park, Kamp Klin is next to the confluence of the Soca and Lepenca rivers, which makes it an ideal base for fishing, kayaking and rafting. The campsite has 50 pitches, all for tourers and with 7A electricity, on one large, grassy field, connected by a circular, gravel access road. It is attractively landscaped with flowers and young trees, which provide some shade. Some pitches are right on the bank of the river (unfenced) and there are beautiful views of the river and the mountains. Kamp Klin is privately owned and there is a 'pension' next door, all run by the Zorc family, who serve the local dishes with compe (potatoes), cottage cheese, grilled trout and local salami in the restaurant. From the site it is only a short drive to the highest point of Slovenia, the Triglav mountain and its beautiful viewpoint with marked walking routes. Like so many Slovenian sites in this area, this is a good holiday base for the active camper.

You might like to know

Kamp Klin is near the world famous Kanin Plateau. The restaurant serves trout freshly caught from the river.

☐ Environmental accreditation
☐ Reduced energy/water consumption policy
☐ Recycling and reusing policy
☐ Information about walking and cycling
☐ Footpaths within 500 m. of the site
☑ Fishing within 1 km.
☐ Riding or pony trekking within 1 km.
☑ Direct river or lake access
☑ Within 10 km. of an area of outstanding natural beauty or national park
☐ Wildlife haven (on site/within 1 km)
☐ Public transport
☐ Dogs welcome

Facilities: One modern toilet block and a further 'Portacabin' style unit with toilets and controllable showers. Laundry with sinks. Bar/restaurant. Play field. Fishing (permit required). Torch useful. Off site: Riding 500 m. Bicycle hire 10 km.

Open: March - October.

Directions: Site is on the main Kranjska Gora - Bovec road and is well signed 3 km. east of Soca. Access is via a sharp turn from the main road and over a small bridge.
GPS: 46.33007, 13.644

Charges guide

Per person	€ 11,00 - € 13,00
child (7-12 yrs)	€ 5,50 - € 6,50
electricity	€ 3,50

Park Grubhof

Nr. 39, A-5092 Saint Martin bei Lofer (Salzburg)
t: 065 888 237 e: home@grubhof.com
alanrogers.com/AU0265 www.grubhof.com

Accommodation: ☑ Pitch ☑ Mobile home/chalet ☑ Hotel/B&B ☐ Apartment

Park Grubhof is a well organised, spacious site in a very scenic riverside location. The 200 pitches all with 12A electricity, have been carefully divided into separate areas for different types of visitor – dog owners, young people, families and groups, and a quiet area. There are 150 very large pitches, all with electricity, water and drainage, along the bank of the Saalach river. Although new, the central building housing reception, a cosy inn, a shop with caféteria, as well as a super sauna and wellness area and some of the site's sanitary facilities, has been built in traditional Tirolian style using, in part, materials hundreds of years old reclaimed from old farmhouses. The result is most attractive. Some areas are wooded with plenty of shade, others are more open and there are some very attractive log cabins which have been rescued from the old logging camps. Many of the possible activities are based around the river, where you will find barbecue areas, canoeing and white water rafting, fishing and swimming (when the river level reduces).

Special offers
Low season discount packages include guided walks, sauna and spa entrance. Special offers for couples.

You might like to know
This spacious site bordering the Berchtesgaden national park is set in unspoilt countryside and has outstanding facilities and spectacular Alpine scenery.

☑ Environmental accreditation
☐ Reduced energy/water consumption policy
☐ Recycling and reusing policy
☑ Information about walking and cycling
☑ Footpaths within 500 m. of the site
☑ Fishing within 1 km.
☐ Riding or pony trekking within 1 km.
☑ Direct river or lake access
☑ Within 10 km. of an area of outstanding natural beauty or national park
☐ Wildlife haven (on site/within 1 km)
☑ Public transport
☑ Dogs welcome

Facilities: Two attractive, modern sanitary units give a good provision of all facilities. Large showers. Some washbasins in cubicles. Saunas, steam bath, massage, fitness room. Separate facilities for canoeists. Motorcaravan services. Shop, restaurant and bar. WiFi. Playground. Games room. Children's playroom. Watersports. Cabins to rent. Hotel and B&B accommodation. Off site: Cross-country track 300 m. Swimming pools at Lofer (open all day in summer) 1 km. Skiing at Lofer Alm 2 km. Gorges and caves 5-7 km. Salzburg 40 minutes drive. Marked walking and cycling trails. Mountain climbing.

Open: All year.

Directions: From A12 exit 17 (south of Kufstein) take B178 east to St Johann in Tyrol, then continue on the B178 northwest to Lofer, then south on B311 towards Zell am See. Site is 200 m. after the Lagerhaus filling station on the left. GPS: 47.57498, 12.70497

Charges guide

Per unit incl. 2 persons and electricity	€ 20,00 - € 29,00
extra person	€ 5,70 - € 7,20
child (under 14 yrs)	€ 3,70 - € 4,50
dog	€ 3,00

No credit cards.

Camping de la Croix Saint Martin

Allée du Camping, 99 avenue des Graviers, F-03200 Abrest (Allier)
t: 04 70 32 67 74 e: camping-vichy@orange.fr
alanrogers.com/FR03110 www.camping-vichy.com

Accommodation: ☑Pitch ☑Mobile home/chalet ☐ Hotel/B&B ☐ Apartment

La Croix Saint Martin is in Abrest on the edge of the attractive spa town of Vichy and close to the Bourbonnais mountains. The site is on the right bank of the Allier and extends over 3 hectares of wooded parkland. There are 90 level grassy pitches with 75 for touring and 45 with 10A electricity. They are separated by some hedging and a variety of mature trees give varying amounts of shade. Vichy's elegant parks are less than 30 minutes on foot and the town centre is only another ten minutes. No twin axle caravans. On site amenities include volleyball, tennis table tennis, boules and a small swimming pool. Various activities are held on site during the peak season, including a children's club and occasional communal meals. Canoeing is popular on the Allier and in the high season. Canoe trips to nearby St Yorre and Ris are available. A popular farmer's market is held in the village of Abrest every week. Other shops are within easy access including the Centre Commercial du Carré d'As, on the other bank of the Allier.

You might like to know
It is possible to reach the summit of an Auvergne volcano on a one-hour excursion and enjoy the breathtaking landscape.

☐ Environmental accreditation
☐ Reduced energy/water consumption policy
☐ Recycling and reusing policy
☑ Information about walking and cycling
☑ Footpaths within 500 m. of the site
☐ Fishing within 1 km.
☐ Riding or pony trekking within 1 km.
☐ Direct river or lake access
☐ Within 10 km. of an area of outstanding natural beauty or national park
☑ Wildlife haven (on site/within 1 km)
☐ Public transport
☑ Dogs welcome

Facilities: Adequate toilet block with all necessary facilities. Swimming pool (1/5–30/9). Fishing. Play area. Volleyball. Table tennis, tennis, boules. Children's miniclub (July/Aug). Tourist information. Motorcaravan services. Free wifi. Off site: Vichy centre 40 minutes walk. Bus to Vichy. Canoeing, windsurfing, river bathing 3 km. Walking, cycling and riding in the Auvergne.

Open: 1 April - 31 October.

Directions: Abrest lies just south of Vichy. From town centre, head south D906 (Avenue de Thiers) to Abrest. Follow signs to site. GPS: 46.1073, 3.43747

Charges guide

Per unit incl. 2 persons and electricity	€ 14,60 - € 18,90
extra person	€ 3,70 - € 4,90
child (under 7 yrs)	€ 2,50 - € 3,50

Camping des Princes d'Orange

F-05700 Orpierre (Hautes-Alpes)
t: 04 92 66 22 53 e: campingorpierre@wanadoo.fr
alanrogers.com/FR05000 www.campingorpierre.com

Accommodation: ☑Pitch ☑Mobile home/chalet ☐ Hotel/B&B ☐ Apartment

This attractive, terraced site, set on a hillside above the village has been thoughtfully developed. Muriel, the owner, speaks excellent English and the genuine, friendly welcome means many families return year upon year, bringing in turn new generations. Divided into five terraces, each with its own toilet block, some of its 100 generously sized pitches (96 for touring) enjoy good shade from trees and have electricity connections (10A). In high season, one terrace is reserved as a one-star camping area for young people. Whether you choose to drive, climb, walk or cycle, there is plenty of wonderful scenery to discover in the immediate vicinity, whilst not far away, some exhilarating hang-gliding and parascending can be enjoyed. It is renowned as a world class rock climbing venue, with over 600 climbing routes in the surrounding mountains. For those seeking to 'get away from it all' in an area of outstanding natural beauty, there can be few more tranquil sites.

You might like to know

Orpierre is at the crossroads of three magnificent regions, which enjoy an abundance of sunshine. Discover the natural and man-made features of the southern alpes on one of the organised high season treks.

☐ Environmental accreditation
☐ Reduced energy/water consumption policy
☐ Recycling and reusing policy
☑ Information about walking and cycling
☑ Footpaths within 500 m. of the site
☐ Fishing within 1 km.
☐ Riding or pony trekking within 1 km.
☑ Direct river or lake access
☑ Within 10 km. of an area of outstanding natural beauty or national park
☑ Wildlife haven (on site/within 1 km)
☐ Public transport
☑ Dogs welcome

Facilities: Six well equipped toilet blocks. Baby bath. Laundry facilities. Bread. Bar (1/4-31/10). Heated swimming pool and paddling pool (15/6-15/9). Play area with inflatable climbing tower. Boules. Games room. Fridge hire. Only gas barbecues are permitted. Free WiFi around reception area. Off site: Orpierre with a few shops and bicycle hire 500 m. Fishing 7 km. Nearest shopping centre Laragne 12 km. Riding 19 km. Hang-gliding. Parascending. Rock climbing. Walking. Mountain biking. Gorges de Guil.

Open: 1 April - 31 October.

Directions: Turn off N75 road at Eyguians onto D30 - site is signed on left at crossroads in the centre of Orpierre village.
GPS: 44.31121, 5.69677

Charges guide

Per unit incl. 2 persons and electricity	€ 21,10 - € 27,70
extra person	€ 5,50 - € 7,80
child (under 7 yrs)	€ 3,00 - € 3,70
dog	€ 1,70

No credit cards.

Camping Domaine de la Bergerie

1330 chemin de la Sine, F-06140 Vence (Alpes-Maritimes)

t: **04 93 58 09 36** e: info@camping-domainedelabergerie.com

alanrogers.com/FR06030 www.camping-domainedelabergerie.com

Accommodation: ☑Pitch ☑Mobile home/chalet ☐ Hotel/B&B ☐ Apartment

La Bergerie is a quiet, family owned site that celebrates its 60th anniversary in 2012. It is situated in the hills 3 km. from Vence and 10 km. from the sea at Cagnes-sur-Mer. An extensive, natural, lightly wooded site, it is in a secluded position at about 300 m. above sea level. Most of the pitches are shaded and all are of a good size. There are 450 pitches, 245 with electricity (2/5A), including 65 also with water and drainage. Because of the nature of this site, some areas are a little distance from the toilet blocks. With the aim of keeping this a quiet and tranquil place to stay, there are no organised activities and definitely no groups accepted. A warden is available near the entrance to deal with anything when reception is closed and there are security guards in July and August. A well stocked shop sells all the essentials, some products of the region and takes orders for bread. Grasse, the famous perfume centre, is only 25 km. away. There are many places to visit in this area and things to do, information is available in reception.

Special offers

Low season offers include: less 10% for stays over 10 nights; in high season: less 15% for stays over 25 nights. Charges are 20% lower 25 March-30 April when facilities are closed.

You might like to know

Ideal for discovering the Cote d'Azur: Nice, Antibes, Cannes, Monaco; and just inland: Grasse, St Paul de Vence, Gourdon, the Parc National du Mercantour and its Parc aux Loups (Wolf Park) and much more.

☐ Environmental accreditation
☐ Reduced energy/water consumption policy
☑ Recycling and reusing policy
☑ Information about walking and cycling
☑ Footpaths within 500 m. of the site
☐ Fishing within 1 km.
☐ Riding or pony trekking within 1 km.
☐ Direct river or lake access
☐ Within 10 km. of an area of outstanding natural beauty or national park
☑ Wildlife haven (on site/within 1 km)
☑ Public transport
☑ Dogs welcome

Facilities: Refurbished toilet blocks are centrally positioned and include excellent provision for disabled visitors (pitches near the block are reserved for disabled visitors). Good shop. Small bar/restaurant, takeaway (all 1/5-30/9). Large swimming pool and smaller pool, spacious sunbathing area (1/5-30/9). Playground. Tennis. 12 shaded boules pitches (lit at night) with competitions in season. Charcoal barbecues are not permitted. Two mobile home and new camping 'pods' to rent. Off site: Bus to Vence 300 m. from entrance (bus comes to site in July and Aug). Beach at Cagnes-sur-Mer 10 km. Riding and fishing 10 km. Golf 18 km. Grasse, famous perfume centre 25 km.

Open: 25 March - 15 October.

Directions: From A8 exit 48 take Cagnes-sur-Mer road towards Vence (do not follow Satnav instructions to turn off this road before you reach Vence). At first roundabout in Vence follow signs for Centre Ville and site is well signed from here. GPS: 43.71174, 7.0905

Charges guide

Per unit incl. 2 persons and electricity (2A)	€ 20,00 - € 27,50
extra person	€ 5,00
child (3-7 yrs)	€ 3,50

Kawan Village les Genêts

Lac de Pareloup, F-12410 Salles-Curan (Aveyron)
t: 05 65 46 35 34 e: contact@camping-les-genets.fr
alanrogers.com/FR12080 www.camping-les-genets.fr

Accommodation: ☑Pitch ☑Mobile home/chalet ☐ Hotel/B&B ☐ Apartment

The 163 pitches include 80 grassy, mostly individual pitches for touring units. These are in two areas, one on each side of the entrance lane, and are divided by hedges, shrubs and trees. Most have electricity (6A) and many also have water and waste water drain. The site slopes gently down to the beach and lake with facilities for all watersports including water skiing. A full animation and activities programme is organised in high season, and there is much to see and do in this very attractive corner of Aveyron. This family run site is on the shores of Lac de Pareloup and offers both family holiday and watersports facilities. Used by tour operators (25 pitches). The site is not suitable for American style motorhomes.

You might like to know

A number of farms close to the campsite welcome visitors, and you can sample some of the tempting local produce at one of the many markets.

- ☑ Environmental accreditation
- ☑ Reduced energy/water consumption policy
- ☑ Recycling and reusing policy
- ☑ Information about walking and cycling
- ☐ Footpaths within 500 m. of the site
- ☑ Fishing within 1 km.
- ☐ Riding or pony trekking within 1 km.
- ☑ Direct river or lake access
- ☐ Within 10 km. of an area of outstanding natural beauty or national park
- ☐ Wildlife haven (on site/within 1 km)
- ☐ Public transport
- ☑ Dogs welcome

Facilities: Two sanitary units, one refurbished, with suite for disabled guests. Baby room. Laundry. Well stocked shop (from 1/6). Bar, restaurant, snacks (14/6-5/9). Swimming pool, spa pool (from 1/6; unsupervised). Playground. Minigolf. Boules. Bicycle hire. Pedaloes, windsurfers, kayaks. Fishing licences available. WiFi in bar.

Open: 21 May - 11 September.

Directions: From Salles-Curan take D577 for about 4 km. and turn right into a narrow lane immediately after a sharp right hand bend. Site is signed at junction. GPS: 44.18933, 2.76693

Charges guide

Per unit incl. 2 persons and electricity	€ 18,00 - € 40,00
extra person	€ 4,00 - € 8,00
child (2-7 yrs)	free - € 7,00
pet	€ 3,00 - € 4,00

Camping le Muret

F-12200 Saint Salvadou (Aveyron)
t: 05 65 81 80 69 e: info@lemuret.com
alanrogers.com/FR12300 www.lemuret.com

Accommodation: ☑Pitch ☑Mobile home/chalet ☐ Hotel/B&B ☐ Apartment

The owners, Alain and Annette Larroque, bought this 40 year old campsite in 2006 and are making improvements, such as a new restaurant and appointing their own chef. A very peaceful site, the loudest noise you are likely to hear is the sound of croaking frogs and the birds singing. There are 43 pitches (40 for touring), 3 chalets and equipped tents for rent. They are large (120-200 sq.m.) and all on grass, with dividing hedges and ample shade given by mature trees. You can be assured of a relaxing time here in the heart of the countryside. There is good company in the evening in the bar and restaurant. New gites have been introduced, finished to a very high standard.

You might like to know

Le Muret is located about 15 km. from the village of Villefranche de Rouergue with its magnificent and famous royal castle. It is well worth visiting.

☐ Environmental accreditation
☐ Reduced energy/water consumption policy
☐ Recycling and reusing policy
☑ Information about walking and cycling
☐ Footpaths within 500 m. of the site
☑ Fishing within 1 km.
☑ Riding or pony trekking within 1 km.
☑ Direct river or lake access
☐ Within 10 km. of an area of outstanding natural beauty or national park
☑ Wildlife haven (on site/within 1 km)
☐ Public transport
☑ Dogs welcome

Facilities: Single sex toilet block with both Turkish and British style toilets. Facilities for disabled visitors. Washing machine. Small shop for basics. New bar and restaurant. Lake for swimming and fishing. Play area on grass. Barbecue area. Activities for children in high season. Musicians weekly in high season. Torches useful. Off site: Riding 1 km. Golf and bicycle hire 16 km.

Open: 1 April - 31 October.

Directions: From the A20 exit 56 (Bastide, Murat, Rodez) take the D802 (Rodez, Decazeville, Figeac). In Figeac take D822 to Villefranche-de-Rouergue. From Villefranche take D911 towards Rieupeyroux. Site is clearly signed (towards Saint Salvadou). For caravans continue on the D911 for 7.5 km. before turning right at the Solville crossroads (Carmaux D905A) and follow signs to site (5 km). GPS: 44.26680, 2.11580

Charges guide

Per unit incl. 2 persons and electricity	€ 19,00 - € 20,50
extra person	€ 2,70 - € 3,50
child (2- yrs)	€ 1,80 - € 3,50
dog	€ 1,80 - € 2,50

Camping la Vallée Heureuse

Impasse Lavau, F-13660 Orgon (Bouches du Rhône)
t: 04 90 44 17 13   e: information@camping-lavalleeheureuse.com
alanrogers.com/FR13310   www.camping-lavalleeheureuse.com

Accommodation: ☑ Pitch ☑ Mobile home/chalet ☐ Hotel/B&B ☐ Apartment

Camping la Vallée Heureuse lies in a valley in the beautiful area of Provence close to the A7 Autoroute, between Avignon and Salon-de-Provence. It is close to the parks of the Cévennes, the Carmargue and the Lubéron making it an ideal centre for touring this very interesting region, as well as the coast a little further south. The site is terraced with 80 stony grassy pitches, some quite large and many with shade and 16A electricity. Good for large outfits. There is a bar, swimming and paddling pools with a sunbathing area, ideal for unwinding at the end of a day exploring the region. Around the site are many marked footpaths and cycle tracks and close by are cliffs which are internationally famous for climbing. At the foot of the cliffs is an attractive lake. There are several medieval villages with their châteaux and fortified towers. Cavaillon, famous for its melons and colourful Provençal market is only 3 km. to the south. The famous historical cities of Avignon and Arles are within easy driving distance.

You might like to know

The generous owners may present you with a bottle of their own wine on the first day of your stay.

☐ Environmental accreditation
☑ Reduced energy/water consumption policy
☑ Recycling and reusing policy
☐ Information about walking and cycling
☑ Footpaths within 500 m. of the site
☐ Fishing within 1 km.
☐ Riding or pony trekking within 1 km.
☐ Direct river or lake access
☐ Within 10 km. of an area of outstanding natural beauty or national park
☑ Wildlife haven (on site/within 1 km)
☐ Public transport
☑ Dogs welcome

Facilities: Modern toilet block with all necessary facilities. Small shop. Swimming and paddling pools. Solarium. Children's play area. Table tennis. Minigolf. Boules. TV room. Internet point and WiFi. Entertainment programme and children's club. Off site: Restaurant and snacks 1 km. Lake swimming and fishing close by. Rock climbing walls. Many marked footpaths and cycle routes. Cavaillon 3 km. l'Isle-sur-la-Sorgue (antiques). St Rémy 15 km. Avignon 25 km.

Open: 1 April - 15 September.

Directions: Leave A7 autoroute, exit 25, signed St Rémy-de-Provence. Shortly, at roundabout, take D26 to Orgon. Site is well signed to the south of the village. GPS: 43.781891, 5.040225

Charges guide

Per unit incl. 2 persons and electricity	€ 18,80 - € 22,50
dog	€ 1,50 - € 1,70

Camping Antioche d'Oléron

Route de Proires, F-17840 La Brée-les-Bains (Charente-Maritime)
t: 05 46 47 92 00 e: info@camping-antiochedoleron.com
alanrogers.com/FR17570 www.camping-antiochedoleron.com

Accommodation: ☑ Pitch ☑ Mobile home/chalet ☐ Hotel/B&B ☐ Apartment

Situated to the northeast of the island, Camping Antioche is quietly located within a five minute walk of the beach. There are 130 pitches, of which 73 are occupied by mobile homes and 57 are for touring units. The pitches are set amongst attractive shrubs and palm trees and all have electricity (10A), water and a drain. A new pool area which comprises two swimming pools (heated), two jacuzzis, two paddling pools and a raised sunbathing deck, is beautifully landscaped with palms and flowers. A small bar, restaurant and takeaway offer reasonably priced food and drinks. The site becomes livelier in season with regular evening entertainment and activities for all the family. With specially prepared trails for cycling, and oyster farms and salt flats to visit, the Ile d'Oléron offers something for everyone. Bresnais market, selling local produce and products, is within easy access on foot and is held daily in high season.

You might like to know
Located in the north of the island, the Saumonards forest and the dramatic Pointe Chassiron are two popular destinations for visitors and can be reached on foot or by bicycle.

- ☐ Environmental accreditation
- ☑ Reduced energy/water consumption policy
- ☑ Recycling and reusing policy
- ☑ Information about walking and cycling
- ☑ Footpaths within 500 m. of the site
- ☑ Fishing within 1 km.
- ☐ Riding or pony trekking within 1 km.
- ☐ Direct river or lake access
- ☑ Within 10 km. of an area of outstanding natural beauty or national park
- ☐ Wildlife haven (on site/within 1 km)
- ☐ Public transport
- ☑ Dogs welcome

Facilities: The single sanitary block is of a good standard and is kept clean and fresh. Facilities for disabled visitors. Laundry. Motorcaravan services. Bar, restaurant and snack bar (weekends only May and June, daily July/Aug). Swimming and paddling pools. Games room. Play area. WiFi. Bicycle hire (July/Aug). Off site: Beach and fishing 150 m. Riding 1.5 km. Golf 7 km.

Open: 1 April - 30 September.

Directions: Cross the bridge on the D26 and join the D734. After St Georges turn right onto the D273E1 towards La Brée-les-Baines. At T-junction turn left from where the campsite is signed. GPS: 46.02007, -1.35764

Charges guide

Per unit incl. 2 persons and electricity	€ 22,30 - € 37,30
extra person	€ 7,50 - € 8,70
child (1-14 yrs)	€ 4,20 - € 5,40
dog	€ 4,20

Camping Au Bois de Calais

Rue Rene Cassin, F-19800 Corrèze (Corrèze)
t: 05 55 26 26 27 e: auboisdecalais@orange.fr
alanrogers.com/FR19170 www.auboisdecalais.com

Accommodation: ☑Pitch ☑Mobile home/chalet ☐ Hotel/B&B ☐ Apartment

The name of this site may be misleading – it's nowhere near Calais. Au Bois de Calais is actually located within the Parc Naturel Régional de Millevaches in the Limousin. This is a holiday centre comprising a campsite, chalets, gites and mobile homes. The 30 touring pitches are very large (minimum 100 sq.m) and all have water and electricity. On-site amenities include a bar and restaurant (with terrace), and a shop specialising in local produce. Sports amenities include a swimming pool and volleyball. There is also a small fishing pond, with the River Corrèze running along one side of the site. The Plateau de Millevaches is a vast region of lakes and forests, extending towards the Auvergne, with miles of cycle trails and hiking tracks. This is an isolated and relatively uninhabited area but with a great deal to discover. The Mont Bessou, for example, is the highest point, at 1001 metres, with fine views to the Auvergne and Cantal. The Cascades de Gimel are spectacular waterfalls with an overall drop of 143 metres.

Facilities: Bar. Restaurant. Shop. Swimming pool. Fishing pond. Basketball. Play area. Activities and entertainment programme. Tourist information. Chalets, mobile homes and gites for rent. Off site: Walking and cycle tracks. Riding. Parc Naturel Régional de Millevaches.

Open: 1 April - 31 October.

Directions: Site is north of Tulle. Approaching from Tulle, head east on A89 and leave at exit 21. Then, head north on D1089 and D26 to Corrèze from here follow signs to the site. GPS: 45.364886, 1.871006

Charges guide

Per unit incl. 2 persons and electricity	€ 18,00 - € 23,50
dog	€ 2,00

You might like to know

A little corner of paradise! Le Bois de Calais campsite lies in a protected area of the Millevaches national park in Limousin, and is a holder of the European Ecolabel.

- ☑ Environmental accreditation
- ☑ Reduced energy/water consumption policy
- ☑ Recycling and reusing policy
- ☑ Information about walking and cycling
- ☑ Footpaths within 500 m. of the site
- ☑ Fishing within 1 km.
- ☐ Riding or pony trekking within 1 km.
- ☑ Direct river or lake access
- ☑ Within 10 km. of an area of outstanding natural beauty or national park
- ☑ Wildlife haven (on site/within 1 km)
- ☑ Public transport
- ☑ Dogs welcome

Les Hameaux du Perrier

F-19600 Lissac-sur-Couze (Corrèze)
t: 05 55 84 34 48 e: info@chalets-en-france.com
alanrogers.com/FR19190 www.chalets-en-france.com

Accommodation: ☐ Pitch ☑ Mobile home/chalet ☐ Hotel/B&B ☐ Apartment

Les Hameaux du Perrier is a member of the Chalets en France group. This group comprises four chalet parks in southern France. Please note, however, that there are no touring pitches here. The site is open all year and can be found 10 minutes southwest of Brive-la-Gaillarde on the border between the Corrèze and Dordogne départements. The site enjoys fine views of the large Lac du Couze, popular for sailing and windsurfing. On-site amenities include two swimming pools and a bar/restaurant. During the peak season, there is a children's club and various other activities. Accommodation on offer here is an attractive range of 94 wooden chalets, thoughtfully dispersed around the site.

You might like to know

Discover the region on some of the excursions organised by the campsite and accompanied by qualified staff.

☐ Environmental accreditation
☐ Reduced energy/water consumption policy
☐ Recycling and reusing policy
☑ Information about walking and cycling
☑ Footpaths within 500 m. of the site
☐ Fishing within 1 km.
☐ Riding or pony trekking within 1 km.
☐ Direct river or lake access
☐ Within 10 km. of an area of outstanding natural beauty or national park
☑ Wildlife haven (on site/within 1 km)
☐ Public transport
☑ Dogs welcome

Facilities: Bar. Restaurant. Takeaway. Two swimming pools. Play area. Multisport pitch. Games room. Tourist information. Entertainment and activity programme. Children's Club. Chalets for rent. Off site: Lac de Couze 500 m. Sailing and windsurfing. Fishing. Cycle and walking trails. Riding. Brive (large town with many shops and restaurants).

Open: All year.

Directions: Take exit 51 from the A20 motorway (Brive south) and then head west on the D59 to Lissac sur Couze. The site is well signed upon arrival at the village. GPS: 45.10029, 1.43848

Charges guide

Contact the site for details.

Les Hameaux de Miel

F-19190 Beynat (Corrèze)
t: 05 55 84 34 48 e: info@chalets-en-france.com
alanrogers.com/FR19200 www.chalets-en-france.com

Accommodation: ☐ Pitch ☑ Mobile home/chalet ☐ Hotel/B&B ☐ Apartment

Les Hameaux de Miel is a member of the Chalets en France group, which comprises six chalet parks in southern France. Please note, however, that there are no touring pitches here. The site is open all year and has a hilltop location with fine views of the surrounding valleys and forests of the Limousin. The Etang de Miel is three minutes walk away and has received the European blue flag accreditation for its cleanliness. The lake is ideal for sailing and windsurfing, as well as fishing, and also has special facilities for disabled visitors. A children's club operates during the peak season and various other activities are organised including archery, rock climbing and riding. Chalets here are attractively dispersed around the site and are all available for rent. Bread and pastries can be delivered to your door each morning. The site makes a good base to explore the surrounding Correze area. The Dordogne and Lot rivers provide many opportunities for fishing, canoeing, walking and sightseeing.

You might like to know
Situated on a hilltop at an altitude of 520 m. the site enjoys some wonderful views of the surrounding countryside.

- ☐ Environmental accreditation
- ☐ Reduced energy/water consumption policy
- ☑ Recycling and reusing policy
- ☑ Information about walking and cycling
- ☑ Footpaths within 500 m. of the site
- ☐ Fishing within 1 km.
- ☐ Riding or pony trekking within 1 km.
- ☐ Direct river or lake access
- ☐ Within 10 km. of an area of outstanding natural beauty or national park
- ☑ Wildlife haven (on site/within 1 km)
- ☐ Public transport
- ☑ Dogs welcome

Facilities: Two swimming pools (one covered in low season). Play area. Multisports pitch. Volleyball. Games room. Entertainment and activity programme. Children's Club. Chalets for rent. Tourist information. Off site: Etang de Miel 300 m. Fishing 500 m. Golf, boat launching and sailing 5 km. Cycling and walking trails.

Open: All year.

Directions: Take exit 50 from the A20 motorway (Brive) and then head east on the N89 to Malemort sur Correze. Shortly beyond this town, join the southbound D921 to Beynat. The site is beyond the town and is well signed. GPS: 45.12932, 1.76141

Charges guide

Contact the site for details.

Les Cottages du Puy d'Agnoux

F-19800 Meyrignac l'Eglise (Corrèze)
t: 05 55 84 34 48 e: info@chalets-en-france.com
alanrogers.com/FR19240 www.chalets-en-france.com

Accommodation: ☐ Pitch ☑ Mobile home/chalet ☐ Hotel/B&B ☐ Apartment

This attractive site offers high quality cottage accommodation for up to six persons in the lesser known, but beautiful, Corrèze region to the south west of the Auvergne. The cottages are in a wooded area close to a small lake. The hills and valleys surrounding the site offer a wealth of marked footpaths and cycle routes and will be greatly appreciated by nature lovers. There are many ancient villages, with their old houses, Romanesque churches and local markets, which are well worth visiting. The chalet accommodation, available throughout the year, is spacious and very well equipped. There are three chalets specially equipped for visitors with disabilities. Within 10 km. is Gimel-les-Cascades, a beautiful historic village set out in a wild gorge containing several waterfalls. At the end of July the son-et-lumière display in the medieval châteaux is well worth a visit. The old market town of Tulle with its shops, bars and restaurants and famous for its lace is only 17 km. Treignac with its three ancient castles is also 17 km.

You might like to know

Canoe trips are popular and are organised by the campsite in high season.

☐ Environmental accreditation
☐ Reduced energy/water consumption policy
☑ Recycling and reusing policy
☑ Information about walking and cycling
☑ Footpaths within 500 m. of the site
☑ Fishing within 1 km.
☐ Riding or pony trekking within 1 km.
☑ Direct river or lake access
☐ Within 10 km. of an area of outstanding natural beauty or national park
☑ Wildlife haven (on site/within 1 km)
☐ Public transport
☑ Dogs welcome

Facilities: Laundry room. Bar, restaurant and snack bar. Heated indoor and outdoor swimming pools. Jacuzzi and sauna. Games and TV room. Tennis. Pool table. Playground. Family activities in high season, including a children's miniclub. WiFi. Off site: Minigolf and paintball 2 km. Picturesque old towns and villages. A small range shops in St. Augustine 2 km. Corrèze with Sunday market 3 km. Riding 8 km. Gimel-les-Cascades 10 km. Tulle 17 km. Treignac 17 km. Fishing. Adventure trails in the woods.

Open: All year.

Directions: Leave A89 autoroute at exit 21 northeast of Tulle. Take N89 northeast then the D26 north to Corrèze. Continue through village to site in 2.5 km. GPS: 45.40162, 1.85967

Charges guide

Contact the site for details.

FRANCE – Alèria

Riva Bella Nature Resort & Spa

B.P. 21, F-20270 Alèria (Haute-Corse)
t: 04 95 38 81 10 e: rivabella.corsica@gmail.com
alanrogers.com/FR20040 www.rivabella-corsica.com

Accommodation: ☑ Pitch ☑ Mobile home/chalet ☐ Hotel/B&B ☐ Apartment

This is a relaxed, informal, spacious site alongside an extremely long and beautiful beach. Riva Bella is naturist from 16 May to 19 September only. It offers a variety of pitches situated in beautiful countryside and seaside. The site is divided into several areas with 200 pitches (133 for touring with 6A electricity), some of which are alongside the sandy beach with little shade. Others are in a shady wooded glade on the hillside. The huge fish-laden lakes are a fine feature of this site and a superb balnéotherapy centre offers the very latest beauty and relaxation treatments (men and women) based on marine techniques. The charming owner, Marie Claire Pasqual, is justifiably proud of the site and the fairly unobtrusive rules are designed to ensure that everyone is able to relax, whilst preserving the natural beauty of the environment. Cars are parked away from the pitches. The restaurant offers a sophisticated menu and the excellent beach restaurant/bar has superb sea views.

You might like to know

This beautiful naturist campsite is not far from a sandy beach, perfect for relaxing with your family.

☑ Environmental accreditation
☑ Reduced energy/water consumption policy
☑ Recycling and reusing policy
☑ Information about walking and cycling
☑ Footpaths within 500 m. of the site
☑ Fishing within 1 km.
☑ Riding or pony trekking within 1 km.
☑ Direct river or lake access
☑ Within 10 km. of an area of outstanding natural beauty or national park
☑ Wildlife haven (on site/within 1 km)
☐ Public transport
☑ Dogs welcome

Facilities: High standard toilet facilities. Provision for disabled visitors, children and babies. Laundry. Large shop (15/5-15/10). Fridge hire. Two restaurants with sea and lake views with reasonable prices. Excellent beach restaurant with bar. Watersports, sailing school, pedaloes, fishing. Balnéotherapy centre. Sauna. Aerobics. Giant chess. Archery. Fishing. Riding. Mountain bike hire. Half-court tennis. Walking with llamas. Internet. WiFi (charged). Professional evening entertainment programme. Off site: Tours of the island. Walking. Riding 7 km. Scuba diving 10 km. Paragliding.

Open: All year (naturist 16/5-19/9).

Directions: Site is 12 km. north of Aleria on N198 (Bastia) road. Watch for large signs and unmade road to site and follow for 4 km. GPS: 42.16151, 9.55269

Charges guide

Per unit incl. 2 persons and electricity	€ 23,30 - € 40,30
extra person	€ 5,00 - € 9,00
child (3-8 yrs)	€ 2,00 - € 6,00
dog	€ 2,00 - € 3,50

FRANCE – Saint Pardoux-la-Riviere

Kawan Village Château le Verdoyer

Champs Romain, F-24470 Saint Pardoux-la-Riviere (Dordogne)
t: 05 53 56 94 64 e: chateau@verdoyer.fr
alanrogers.com/FR24010 www.verdoyer.fr

Accommodation: ☑Pitch ☑Mobile home/chalet ☑Hotel/B&B ☐ Apartment

This 26-hectare estate has three lakes, two for fishing and one with a sandy beach and safe swimming area. There are 135 good sized touring pitches, level, terraced and hedged. With a choice of wooded area or open field, all have electricity (5/10A) and most share a water supply between four pitches. There is a swimming pool complex and high season activities are organised for children (5-13 yrs) but there is no disco. This site is well adapted for those with disabilities, with two fully adapted chalets, wheelchair access to all facilities and even a lift into the pool. Château le Verdoyer has been developed in the park of a restored château and is owned by a Dutch family. We particularly like this site for its beautiful buildings and lovely surroundings. It is situated in the lesser known area of the Dordogne sometimes referred to as the Périgord Vert, with its green forests and small lakes. The château itself has rooms to let and its excellent lakeside restaurant is also open to the public.

You might like to know

Château le Verdoyer is situated in the heart of the Parc Naturel Périgord Limousin.

- ☑ Environmental accreditation
- ☑ Reduced energy/water consumption policy
- ☑ Recycling and reusing policy
- ☑ Information about walking and cycling
- ☑ Footpaths within 500 m. of the site
- ☑ Fishing within 1 km.
- ☐ Riding or pony trekking within 1 km.
- ☑ Direct river or lake access
- ☑ Within 10 km. of an area of outstanding natural beauty or national park
- ☐ Wildlife haven (on site/within 1 km)
- ☐ Public transport
- ☑ Dogs welcome

Facilities: Well appointed toilet blocks include facilities for disabled visitors and baby baths. Serviced launderette. Motorcaravan services. Fridge rental. Shop with gas (from 1/5). Bar, snacks, takeaway and restaurant (from 1/5). Bistro (July/Aug). Two pools, the smaller covered in low season, slide, paddling pool. Play areas. Tennis. Minigolf. Bicycle hire. Fishing. Small library. WiFi (charged). Computer in reception for internet access. International newspapers daily. Off site: Riding 5 km. Golf 33 km. 'Circuit des Orchidées' (22 species of orchid). Vélo-rail at Bussière Galant. Market (Thursday and Sunday) at Saint Pardoux 12 km.

Open: 28 April - 30 September.

Directions: Site is 2 km. from the Limoges (N21) - Chalus (D6bis-D85) - Nontron road, 20 km. south of Chalus and is well signed from main road. Site on D96 about 4 km. north of village of Champs Romain. GPS: 45.55035, 0.7947

Charges guide

Per unit incl. 2 persons and electricity	€ 21,00 - € 38,50
extra person	€ 5,00 - € 6,50
child (6-11 yrs)	€ 4,00 - € 5,00
dog	€ 3,00 - € 4,00

Camping le Paradis

Saint Léon-sur-Vézère, F-24290 Montignac (Dordogne)
t: 05 53 50 72 64   e: le-paradis@perigord.com
alanrogers.com/FR24060   www.le-paradis.fr

Accommodation: ☑Pitch ☑Mobile home/chalet ☐ Hotel/B&B ☐ Apartment

Le Paradis is an excellent, very well maintained riverside site, halfway between Les Eyzies and Montignac. The site is landscaped with a variety of mature shrubs and trees. The gardens are beautiful, which gives a wonderful sense of tranquillity. It is very easy to relax on this ecologically friendly site. Systems of reed filters enhance the efficient natural drainage. This is a family run site and you are guaranteed a warm and friendly welcome. There are 200 good sized pitches, with 27 for mobile homes to rent. The pitches are level and with easy access, all with 10A electricity, water and drainage. There are some special pitches for motorcaravans. An excellent restaurant offers a good menu, reasonably priced and using fresh local produce where appropriate. The terraced area outside makes for a convivial family atmosphere. There are many sport and leisure activities. Direct access to the Vézère river for canoeing and swimming is possible at one end of the site. This is a site of real quality, which we thoroughly recommend.

You might like to know

The owners, Ellen and Ge, have carefully selected some colleagues who organise activities such as quad biking from the campsite.

☐ Environmental accreditation
☑ Reduced energy/water consumption policy
☑ Recycling and reusing policy
☑ Information about walking and cycling
☐ Footpaths within 500 m. of the site
☐ Fishing within 1 km.
☑ Riding or pony trekking within 1 km.
☐ Direct river or lake access
☐ Within 10 km. of an area of outstanding natural beauty or national park
☑ Wildlife haven (on site/within 1 km)
☐ Public transport
☑ Dogs welcome

Facilities: High quality, well equipped, heated toilet blocks are kept very clean. Well stocked shop (with gas). Good restaurant, takeaway. Good pool complex heated in low season, paddling pool. Play area. Tennis. BMX track. Multisport court. Canoe hire. Fishing. Bicycle hire. Quad bike and horse riding excursions. WiFi throughout. Large units accepted by arrangement. Mobile homes to rent (no smoking) including one for visitors with disabilities (no dogs permitted). Off site: Riding 3 km.

Open: 1 April - 19 October.

Directions: Site is 12 km. north of Les Eyzies and 3 km. south of St Léon-sur-Vézère, on the east side of the D706. GPS: 45.00207, 1.0711

Charges guide

Per unit incl. 2 persons and electricity	€ 22,10 - € 31,40
extra person	€ 5,60 - € 7,70
child (3-12 yrs)	€ 4,60 - € 6,70
dog	€ 2,50

Domaine de Soleil Plage

Caudon par Montfort, Vitrac, F-24200 Sarlat-la-Canéda (Dordogne)
t: 05 53 28 33 33 e: info@soleilplage.fr
alanrogers.com/FR24090 www.soleilplage.fr

Accommodation: ☑ Pitch ☑ Mobile home/chalet ☐ Hotel/B&B ☐ Apartment

This site is in one of the most attractive sections of the Dordogne valley, with a riverside location. There are 199 pitches, in three sections, with 100 for touring units. Additionally there are 47 mobile homes and 27 chalets for rent. The site offers river swimming from a sizeable sandy bank or there is a very impressive heated pool complex. All pitches are bounded by hedges and are of adequate size with 16A electricity, water and a drain. Most pitches have some shade. If you like a holiday with lots going on, you will enjoy this site. Various activities are organised during high season including walks and sports tournaments, and daily canoe hire is available from the site. Once a week in July and August there is a 'soirée' (charged for) usually involving a barbecue or paella, with band and lots of free wine – worth catching! The site is busy and reservation is advisable. English is spoken. The site is quite expensive in high season and you also pay more for a riverside pitch, but these have fine river views. There is some tour operator presence.

You might like to know

There are numerous caves and castles to explore nearby, including Sarlat (2 km) and Domne (5 km) with original ramparts and gateways.

☐ Environmental accreditation
☐ Reduced energy/water consumption policy
☐ Recycling and reusing policy
☑ Information about walking and cycling
☑ Footpaths within 500 m. of the site
☑ Fishing within 1 km.
☐ Riding or pony trekking within 1 km.
☑ Direct river or lake access
☐ Within 10 km. of an area of outstanding natural beauty or national park
☑ Wildlife haven (on site/within 1 km)
☐ Public transport
☐ Dogs welcome

Facilities: Toilet facilities are in three modern unisex blocks. One has been completely renovated to a high standard with heating and family shower rooms. Laundry facilities. Motorcaravan service point. Well stocked shop, bar with TV and newly refurbished restaurant with local menus and a terrace (all from 1/5). Picnics available to order. Impressive heated main pool, paddling pool, spa pool and two slides. Tennis. Minigolf. Three play areas. Fishing. Canoe and kayak hire. Bicycle hire. Currency exchange. Small library. WiFi throughout (charged). Activities and social events (high season). Off site: Golf 1 km. Riding 5 km. Attractions of the Dordogne.

Open: Easter - 30 September.

Directions: Site is 6 km. south of Sarlat. From A20 take exit 55 (Souillac) towards Sarlat. Follow the D703 to Carsac and on to Montfort. At Montfort castle site is signed on left. Continue for 2 km. down to the river and site. GPS: 44.825, 1.25388

Charges guide

Per unit incl. 2 persons and electricity	€ 21,00 - € 35,50
incl. full services	€ 24,50 - € 50,50
extra person	€ 5,00 - € 7,50
child (2-8 yrs)	€ 3,00 - € 4,50

Castel Camping Saint-Avit Loisirs

Le Bugue, F-24260 Saint Avit-de-Vialard (Dordogne)
t: 05 53 02 64 00 e: contact@saint-avit-loisirs.com
alanrogers.com/FR24180 www.saint-avit-loisirs.com

Accommodation: ☑ Pitch ☑ Mobile home/chalet ☐ Hotel/B&B ☐ Apartment

Although Saint Avit Loisirs is set amidst rolling countryside, far from the hustle and bustle of the main tourist areas of the Dordogne, the facilities are first class, providing virtually everything you could possibly want without the need to leave the site. This makes it ideal for families with children of all ages. The site is in two sections. One part is dedicated to chalets and mobile homes which are available to rent, whilst the main section of the site contains 199 flat and mainly grassy, good sized pitches, 99 for touring units, with electricity (6/10A). With a choice of sun or shade, they are arranged in cul-de-sacs off a main access road and are easily accessible. Environmental friendliness is high on the agenda here and each visitor is provided with a bag with instructions as to what should be placed in it before disposal. Two tour operators are in evidence but their tents and mobile homes are so positioned not to detract in any way from the attractiveness of the surroundings.

You might like to know

Saint-Avit Loisirs is the first Aquitaine site to win the coveted 5-star award.

☑ Environmental accreditation
☑ Reduced energy/water consumption policy
☑ Recycling and reusing policy
☑ Information about walking and cycling
☑ Footpaths within 500 m. of the site
☐ Fishing within 1 km.
☑ Riding or pony trekking within 1 km.
☐ Direct river or lake access
☑ Within 10 km. of an area of outstanding natural beauty or national park
☐ Wildlife haven (on site/within 1 km)
☐ Public transport
☑ Dogs welcome

Facilities: Three modern unisex toilet blocks provide high quality facilities, but could become overstretched in high season. Shop, bar, good quality restaurant, cafeteria. Outdoor swimming pool, children's pool, water slide, 'crazy river', heated indoor pool with jacuzzi, Fitness room. Soundproofed disco. Driving range and putting green. Minigolf. Boules. BMX track. Tennis. Quad bikes. Play area. Bicycle hire. Canoe trips on the Dordogne and other sporting activities organised. Walks and cycle routes from site. Torches useful. Off site: Boulangerie, supermarket, Tuesday market, Birdland (over 500 different species) at Le Bugue 6 km. Medieval town of Sarlat 20 km. Canoeing, golf, riding, fishing nearby.

Open: 2 April - 18 September.

Directions: Site is 6 km. north of Le Bugue. From D710 Le Bugue-Périgueux road, turn west on narrow and bumpy C201 towards St Avit-de-Vialard. Follow road through St Avit, bearing right and site is 1.5 km. GPS: 44.95161, 0.85042

Charges guide

Per unit incl. 2 persons and electricity	€ 18,10 - € 44,00
extra person	€ 3,60 - € 10,20
child (under 4 yrs)	free
dog	€ 2,00 - € 4,90

Camping Caravaning la Bouquerie

F-24590 Saint Geniès-en-Périgord (Dordogne)
t: **05 53 28 98 22** e: **labouquerie@wanadoo.fr**
alanrogers.com/FR24310 www.labouquerie.com

Accommodation: ☑ Pitch ☑ Mobile home/chalet ☐ Hotel/B&B ☐ Apartment

La Bouquerie is situated within easy reach of the main road network in the Dordogne, but without any associated traffic noise. Recent new owners here are investing in new amenities. The main complex is based around some beautifully restored traditional Périgord buildings. There is a bar and restaurant that overlook the impressive pool complex, with a large outdoor terrace for fine weather. The excellent restaurant menu is varied and reasonably priced. Of the 185 pitches, 60 are used for touring units and these are of varying size (80-120 sq.m), flat and grassy, some with shade, and all with 10A electrical connections. The majority of the remainder are for mobile homes and chalets for rent. In high season the site offers a range of sporting activities (aqua-gym, archery, canoeing, walks and more), as well as a children's club each weekday morning. La Bouquerie is ideally situated for exploring the Périgord region, and has something to offer families with children of all ages.

You might like to know

There is an extensive takeaway menu, featuring local dishes and specialities such as foie gras and truffles.

☐ Environmental accreditation
☐ Reduced energy/water consumption policy
☑ Recycling and reusing policy
☑ Information about walking and cycling
☐ Footpaths within 500 m. of the site
☐ Fishing within 1 km.
☐ Riding or pony trekking within 1 km.
☑ Direct river or lake access
☐ Within 10 km. of an area of outstanding natural beauty or national park
☑ Wildlife haven (on site/within 1 km)
☐ Public transport
☑ Dogs welcome

Facilities: Three toilet blocks with facilities for disabled visitors and baby rooms. Washing machines and covered drying lines. Shop. Bar and snacks (all season). Restaurant (12/5-15/9). Takeaway. Heated swimming pool complex including water slides, paddling pool and sunbathing areas with loungers (all season). Carp fishing in lake. Multisport area. Boules. Gym. Paint ball. WiFi (charged). Off site: Shops, restaurants and Sunday market in the nearby village of St Geniès. The prehistoric caves at Lascaus. Museum and animal park at Le Thot. Golf 30 km.

Open: 7 April - 15 September.

Directions: Site is signed on the east side of the D704 Sarlat - Montignac, about 500 m. north of junction with D64 St Geniès road. Turn off D704 at campsite sign and take first left turn signed La Bouquerie. Site is straight ahead. GPS: 44.99865, 1.24549

Charges guide

Per unit incl. 2 persons

and electricity	€ 19,00 - € 25,50
extra person	€ 4,60 - € 6,50
child (under 7 yrs)	€ 3,20 - € 4,50
dog	€ 2,50

FRANCE – Coux-et-Bigaroque

Camping les Valades

D703, F-24220 Coux-et-Bigaroque (Dordogne)
t: 05 53 29 14 27 e: info@lesvalades.com
alanrogers.com/FR24420 www.lesvalades.com

Accommodation: ☑Pitch ☑Mobile home/chalet ☐ Hotel/B&B ☐ Apartment

Sometimes we come across small but beautifully kept campsites which seem to have been a well kept secret, and Les Valades certainly fits the bill. Set on a hillside overlooking lovely countryside between the Dordogne and Vezère rivers, each pitch is surrounded by variety of flowers, shrubs and trees. The 85 pitches are flat and grassy, mostly on terraces, all with 10A electricity and most with individual water and drainage as well. Ten very large pitches (over 300 sq.m) are available for weekly hire, each having a private sanitary unit, dishwashing, fridge and barbecue. At the bottom of the hill, away from the main area, is a swimming pool and a good sized lake for carp fishing, swimming or canoeing (free canoes). Rustic chalets for rent occupy 25 of the largest pitches. From the moment you arrive you can see that the owners, M and Mme Berger, take enormous pride in the appearance of their campsite and there is an abundance of well tended flowers and shrubs everywhere you look.

You might like to know

The Dordogne and Vezère rivers are 5 km. and in the local area you can visit castles, caves, fortified villages, prehistoric shelters and much more. The site organises a large lakeside barbecue – everyone is welcome!

☐ Environmental accreditation
☑ Reduced energy/water consumption policy
☑ Recycling and reusing policy
☑ Information about walking and cycling
☑ Footpaths within 500 m. of the site
☑ Fishing within 1 km.
☐ Riding or pony trekking within 1 km.
☑ Direct river or lake access
☐ Within 10 km. of an area of outstanding natural beauty or national park
☑ Wildlife haven (on site/within 1 km)
☐ Public transport
☑ Dogs welcome

Facilities: Two clean modern toilet blocks, one with family shower rooms. Facilities for disabled people. Washing machine. Shop, bar and restaurant (all July/Aug) and a terrace overlooking the valley. Heated swimming pool (1/6-30/9) with sun terrace and paddling pool. Play area near the lake and pool. Fishing. Canoeing. WiFi (free). Off site: Small shop, bar, restaurant in Coux-et-Bigaroque 5 km. Supermarket at Le Bugue 10 km. Riding and bicycle hire 5 km. Golf 6 km.

Open: 1 April - 15 October.

Directions: Site is signed down a turning on west side of the D703 Le Bugue - Siorac-en-Perigord road, about 3.5 km. north of village of Coux-et-Bigaroque. Turn off D703 and site is 1.5 km. along on right. GPS: 44.86056, 0.96385

Charges guide

Per unit incl. 2 persons	
and electricity	€ 25,00
extra person	€ 6,00
child (under 7 yrs)	€ 4,20
dog	€ 3,15

No credit cards.

Camping le Val d'Ussel

Proissans, F-24200 Sarlat-la-Canéda (Dordogne)
t: 05 53 28 45 22 e: info@homair-vacances.fr
alanrogers.com/FR24430 www.homair.com

Accommodation: ☑ Pitch ☑ Mobile home/chalet ☐ Hotel/B&B ☐ Apartment

Val d'Ussel is in the Perigord-Noir region of France, only 7 km. from the picturesque old town of Sarlat. It is attractively laid out in a wooded parkland setting covering seven hectares giving ample space for everyone. There is a wide range of activities for all the family in the surrounding area and, in the high season, there is plenty to do on the campsite. There are 173 partly sloping, medium sized grass pitches with 40 for touring, the others used for mobiles homes and seasonal use. There is an attractive swimming pool complex ideal for the children and for unwinding after a day sightseeing. The historic market town of Sarlat has an older quarter containing many interesting old houses spanning several centuries. To the south, the River Dordogne meanders through many picture postcard villages well worth visiting. To the west lies the valley of the river Vézère with many caves renowned for their ancient paintings. Numerous watersports can be found on both of these rivers.

Special offers
See the campsite brochure for special camping packages.

You might like to know
This tranquil site in the heart of the countryside has a fishing lake for campers and a children's club in July/August. The bar, restaurant and shop are open from April to September.

☐ Environmental accreditation
☑ Reduced energy/water consumption policy
☑ Recycling and reusing policy
☑ Information about walking and cycling
☑ Footpaths within 500 m. of the site
☑ Fishing within 1 km.
☐ Riding or pony trekking within 1 km.
☐ Direct river or lake access
☑ Within 10 km. of an area of outstanding natural beauty or national park
☑ Wildlife haven (on site/within 1 km)
☐ Public transport
☑ Dogs welcome

Facilities: Minimart. Bar, snack bar, takeaway. Large swimming pool complex. Children's play area. Games/TV room. Table tennis. Boules. Tennis. Fishing. Minigolf. Bicycle hire. Extensive programme of activities organised in the season. WiFi. Off site: Walking and riding organised from site. Many old market towns and villages with their châteaux. Caves. Sarlat 7 km. Watersports on rivers. Marked footpaths and cycle routes.

Open: 2 April - 11 September.

Directions: Leave Sarlat, D704 north towards Montignac. Shortly turn right, signed Proissans and follow signs to site (12 km. north of Sarlat). GPS: 44.936293, 1.232411

Charges guide

Per unit incl. 2 persons and electricity	€ 15,00 - € 20,00

Camping la Sagne

Lieu dit Lassagne, F-24200 Vitrac (Dordogne)
t: 05 53 28 18 36 e: info@camping-la-sagne.com
alanrogers.com/FR24940 www.camping-la-sagne.com

Accommodation: ☑ Pitch ☑ Mobile home/chalet ☐ Hotel/B&B ☐ Apartment

Camping la Sagne is a family run site and is being significantly rebuilt for the 2012 season. The rebuilding programme includes a new reception, bar and snack bar complex and a covered swimming pool and paddling pool with jacuzzi. There are 100 large, level pitches with 70 for touring, all with 16A electricity but long leads are required. Those in the new area will be open and have no shade but those in the older section are separated by hedges and mature trees providing good shade. The site is close to the river Dordogne and access is available via a track down through the trees. Fishing and bathing are possible in the river and canoe trips are organised from the site. There is a programme of entertainment in the high season and all the facilities are open all season.

You might like to know

Built on a former farm, this campsite enjoys a very peaceful and natural setting.

☐ Environmental accreditation
☐ Reduced energy/water consumption policy
☑ Recycling and reusing policy
☐ Information about walking and cycling
☐ Footpaths within 500 m. of the site
☑ Fishing within 1 km.
☐ Riding or pony trekking within 1 km.
☑ Direct river or lake access
☑ Within 10 km. of an area of outstanding natural beauty or national park
☑ Wildlife haven (on site/within 1 km)
☐ Public transport
☑ Dogs welcome

Facilities: One old basic toilet block (refurbishment planned) with all necessary facilities including those for disabled visitors but no washing machine. Small shop. Bar with TV, snack bar and takeaway. Games room. Covered, heated swimming pool, paddling pool and jacuzzi. Fitness room. Children's playground. River fishing and bathing. Wifi near bar (charged). Off site: Golf 800 m. Sarlat with range of shops, bars and restaurants 8 km. Riding 5 km. Bicycle hire 8 km. A good centre for touring the many old market towns with their châteaux and museums. Many marked walks and cycle routes.

Open: 1 May - 30 September.

Directions: Site is 6 km. south of Sarlat. Leave Autoroute A20, exit 55 (Souillac) towards Sarlat. Take D703 to Montfort, turn left following site signs. Site entrance on right in 1 km. GPS: 44.825452, 1.242346

Charges guide

Per unit incl. 2 persons and electricity	€ 19,00 - € 30,00
extra person	€ 5,00 - € 7,00
child (2-13 yrs)	€ 3,00 - € 5,00
dog	€ 4,00 - € 5,00

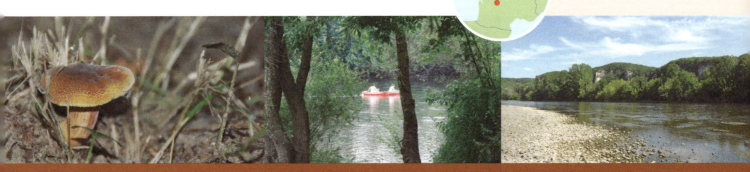

Castel Domaine de Massereau

Les Hauteurs de Sommières, route d'Aubais, F-30250 Sommières (Gard)
t: 04 66 53 11 20   e: info@massereau.fr
alanrogers.com/FR30290   www.massereau.co.uk

Accommodation: ☑ Pitch ☑ Mobile home/chalet ☐ Hotel/B&B ☐ Apartment

A member of the Castels group, de Massereau was opened in August 2006 and is set within a 50-hectare vineyard dating back to 1804. There are now 120 pitches, with 75 available for touring units. Pitch sizes range from 150-250 sq.m. but the positioning of trees on some of the pitches severely limits the useable space. The large modern sanitary block is thoughtfully designed with superb facilities for disabled visitors and children. There is an attractive pool complex and a wide range of leisure facilities. The restaurant offers a reasonable range of good value cuisine and there is a well stocked shop including the vineyard's wines. Amenities include a new, heated swimming pool, a trim trail, mountain bike path and large play area including a trampoline. The camping area is accessed over a narrow bridge (3 m. wide) passing over a section of the 25 km. of cycle routes which enable the surrounding area to be explored safely. A high quality site which is extremely good value for money particularly in the low season.

Special offers
Special low season offer: 16 nights for the price of 14, including four spa sessions (sauna/hammam/jacuzzi).

You might like to know
New for 2012: luxury air-conditioned cottages with a host of features including flat-screen TV, iPod dock, microwave, fridge/freezer. At extra cost: barbecue, WiFi, towels, bedlinen and final clean.

☑ Environmental accreditation
☑ Reduced energy/water consumption policy
☑ Recycling and reusing policy
☑ Information about walking and cycling
☑ Footpaths within 500 m. of the site
☑ Fishing within 1 km.
☑ Riding or pony trekking within 1 km.
☑ Direct river or lake access
☑ Within 10 km. of an area of outstanding natural beauty or national park
☑ Wildlife haven (on site/within 1 km)
☑ Public transport
☑ Dogs welcome

Facilities: The modern toilet block incorporates excellent facilities for children and disabled visitors. Laundry area. Motorcaravan service point. Well stocked shop and newspapers. Restaurant. Bar. Pizzeria and outdoor grill. Takeaway, (all 7/4-30/9). Heated swimming pool with slide. New sauna, steam bath and jacuzzi. Play area. Trampoline. Minigolf. Bicycle hire. Fitness trail. Petanque. Short tennis. TV room. Barbecue hire. Fridge hire. Gas. WiFi. Charcoal barbecues are not allowed. Off site: Fishing and riding 3 km. Golf and sailing 30 km.

Open: 31 March - 10 November.

Directions: From the south on A9 take exit 27 and D12 towards Sommières. Site is 5 km. on right. From the north, there is a width and weight restriction in Sommières. To avoid this remain on the N110 and then take the N2110 into Sommières, crossing the river and turn right onto the D12. Site is on left in 1 km. GPS: 43.765786, 4.097426

Charges guide

Per unit incl. 2 persons and electricity	€ 21,40 - € 41,90
extra person	€ 3,50 - € 10,00
child (under 7 yrs)	€ 2,90 - € 6,50
dog	€ 3,90 - € 5,90

Camping le Moulin

Lieu-dit le Moulin, F-31220 Martres-Tolosane (Haute-Garonne)
t: 05 61 98 86 40 e: info@campinglemoulin.com
alanrogers.com/FR31000 www.campinglemoulin.com

Accommodation: ☑Pitch ☑Mobile home/chalet ☐ Hotel/B&B ☐ Apartment

With attractive shaded pitches and many activities, this family-run campsite has twelve hectares of woods and fields beside the River Garonne. It is close to Martres-Tolosane, an interesting medieval village. Some of the 60 level and grassy pitches are 'supersize' and all have electricity (6-10A). There are 24 chalets to rent. Summer brings opportunities for guided canoeing, archery and walking. A large sports field is available all season, with tennis, volleyball, basketball, boules and birdwatching. Facilities for visitors with disabilities are very good, although the sanitary block is a little dated. Le Moulin is on the site of a 17th-century watermill and the buildings have been traditionally restored. The outdoor bar serves snacks and in summer the restaurant serves full meals. The swimming pool is large with an adjoining children's pool. During the high season, an organised activity and entertainment programme includes a children's club, karaoke, quiz and communal meal nights. Some road noise. A member of Sites et Paysages.

Special offers

On presentation of this guide:
pitch including 2 persons and 6A electricity for just € 16 per night (outside July/August).

You might like to know

This 17th-century, 12-hectare site with its pretty watermill runs alongside the Garonne river. 76 different species of birds have been observed and there are over 40 species of tree, including a famous giant plane tree.

☑ Environmental accreditation
☑ Reduced energy/water consumption policy
☑ Recycling and reusing policy
☑ Information about walking and cycling
☑ Footpaths within 500 m. of the site
☑ Fishing within 1 km.
☐ Riding or pony trekking within 1 km.
☑ Direct river or lake access
☐ Within 10 km. of an area of outstanding natural beauty or national park
☑ Wildlife haven (on site/within 1 km)
☐ Public transport
☑ Dogs welcome

Facilities: Large sanitary block with separate ladies' and gents WCs. Communal area with showers and washbasins in cubicles. Separate heated area for disabled visitors with shower, WC and basin. Baby bath. Laundry facilities. Motorcaravan services. Outdoor bar with WiFi. Snack bar and takeaway (1/6-15/9). Daily bakers van (except Monday). Heated swimming and paddling pools (1/6-15/9). Fishing. Tennis. Canoeing. Archery. Large grounds for dog walking. Walks in the countryside. BMX track. Playground. Games room. Entertainment programme and children's club (high season). Off site: Martres-Tolosane 1.5 km. Walking trails and cycle routes. Riding 4 km. Golf 12 km.

Open: 1 April - 30 September.

Directions: From the A64 (Toulouse-Tarbes) take exit 21 (Boussens) or exit 22 (Martres-Tolosane) and follow signs to Martres-Tolosane. Site is well signed from village. GPS: 43.19048, 1.01788

Charges guide

Per unit incl. 2 persons and electricity	€ 20,00 - € 36,00
extra person	€ 4,50 - € 6,50
child (under 7 yrs)	€ 2,50 - € 3,50
dog	€ 1,50 - € 2,30

Huttopia Rillé

Lac de Rillé, F-37340 Rillé (Indre-et-Loire)
t: 02 47 24 62 97   e: rille@huttopia.com
alanrogers.com/FR37140   www.huttopia.com

Accommodation: ☑ Pitch   ☑ Mobile home/chalet   ☐ Hotel/B&B   ☐ Apartment

Huttopia Rillé is rural site ideal for tent campers seeking a more natural, environmentally friendly, peaceful campsite close to a lake. Cars are parked outside the barrier but allowed on site to unload and load. The 146 slightly uneven and sloping pitches, 80 for touring, are scattered between the pine trees. All have 10A electricity (very long leads needed) and 24 are fully serviced. They vary in size and are numbered but not marked. This site is designed for those with tents, though small caravans and motorhomes (special area) are accepted. It is not ideal for those with walking difficulties. Communal barbecues only. The site is situated in an area ideal for exploring and there are numerous marked footpaths and cycle tracks close by. The area north of the lake, in easy reach of the site, is designated a nature reserve offering excellent opportunities for birdwatching. After a long day exploring the region, you can unwind with a refreshing drink or a light meal on the terrace overlooking the lake and small swimming pool.

You might like to know

Home to the beautiful châteaux of the Loire, this area also has some lush forests rich in flora and fauna.

- ☑ Environmental accreditation
- ☑ Reduced energy/water consumption policy
- ☑ Recycling and reusing policy
- ☑ Information about walking and cycling
- ☑ Footpaths within 500 m. of the site
- ☑ Fishing within 1 km.
- ☐ Riding or pony trekking within 1 km.
- ☑ Direct river or lake access
- ☐ Within 10 km. of an area of outstanding natural beauty or national park
- ☑ Wildlife haven (on site/within 1 km)
- ☐ Public transport
- ☑ Dogs welcome

Facilities: Modern central toilet block with family rooms and facilities for disabled visitors (no ramps and difficult access for wheelchairs). A smaller block has separate showers, washbasins and facilities for disabled visitors. Motorcaravan service point. Small heated swimming pool with paddling area (May-Sept). Play area. Fishing. Canoes on lake. Communal barbecue areas. Max. 1 dog. Off site: Small steam train passes site. Several châteaux to visit. Many marked walks and cycle tracks. Nature reserve at the lake. Riding 6 km. Golf 15 km.

Open: 22 April - 6 November.

Directions: Rillé is 40 km. west of Tours. Leave D766 Angers - Blois road at Château la Vallière take D749 southwest. In Rillé turn west on D49. Site is on right in 2 km. GPS: 47.45811, 0.2192

Charges guide

Per unit incl. 2 persons and electricity	€ 20,20 - € 31,90
extra person	€ 5,30 - € 7,10
child (2-7 yrs)	€ 3,20 - € 4,75
dog	€ 4,00

Camping de Surchauffant

Le Pont de la Pyle, F-39270 La Tour-du-Meix (Jura)
t: 03 84 25 41 08 e: info@camping-surchauffant.fr
alanrogers.com/FR39020 www.camping-surchauffant.fr

Accommodation: ☑ Pitch ☑ Mobile home/chalet ☐ Hotel/B&B ☐ Apartment

With only 180 pitches, this site may appeal to those who prefer a more informal atmosphere, however it can be lively in high season. It is pleasantly situated above the beaches bordering the Lac de Vouglans, which can be reached quickly on foot directly from the site. The 133 touring pitches are of a reasonable size and are informally arranged, some are fully serviced and most with electricity (5A). They are divided by hedges and there is some shade. The lake offers a variety of watersports activities, boat trips, etc. and is used for fishing and swimming (guarded in high season as it shelves steeply). Two signposted walks start from within 100 m. of the site entrance. English is spoken.

Special offers

7 nights for the price of 6 in April, May, June and September.

You might like to know

You can try the 13 km. circuit starting from the site by mountain bike or on foot, or take a boat across the lake from the sailing school.

☐ Environmental accreditation
☐ Reduced energy/water consumption policy
☐ Recycling and reusing policy
☑ Information about walking and cycling
☑ Footpaths within 500 m. of the site
☑ Fishing within 1 km.
☐ Riding or pony trekking within 1 km.
☑ Direct river or lake access
☑ Within 10 km. of an area of outstanding natural beauty or national park
☑ Wildlife haven (on site/within 1 km)
☐ Public transport
☑ Dogs welcome

Facilities: The sanitary facilities are older in style and adequate rather than luxurious, but reasonably well maintained and clean when we visited. They include some washbasins in private cabins. Laundry. Heated swimming pool, paddling pool and surround (15/6-15/9). Three playgrounds. Entertainment (July/Aug). Safety deposit boxes. Off site: Bicycle hire or riding 5 km. Restaurant, takeaway and shops adjacent.

Open: 24 April - 15 September.

Directions: From A39 take exit 7 and N1082 to Lons-le-Saunier. Continue south on D52 for about 20 km. to Orgelet. Site is by the D470, at La Tour-du-Meix, about 4 km. east of Orgelet. GPS: 46.5231, 5.67401

Charges guide

Per unit incl. 2 persons and electricity	€ 15,00 - € 23,50
extra person (over 4 yrs)	€ 2,50 - € 4,70
dog	€ 1,00 - € 1,60

Leading Camping les Alicourts

Domaine des Alicourts, F-41300 Pierrefitte-sur-Sauldre (Loir-et-Cher)
t: 02 54 88 63 34 e: info@lesalicourts.com
alanrogers.com/FR41030 www.lesalicourts.com

Accommodation: ☑Pitch ☑Mobile home/chalet ☐ Hotel/B&B ☐ Apartment

A secluded holiday village set in the heart of the forest, with many sporting facilities and a super spa centre, Parc des Alicourts is midway between Orléans and Bourges, to the east of the A71. There are 490 pitches, 150 for touring and the remainder occupied by mobile homes and chalets. All pitches have electricity connections (6A) and good provision for water, and most are 150 sq.m. Locations vary, from wooded to more open areas, thus giving a choice of amount of shade. All facilities are open all season and the leisure amenities are exceptional. The Senseo Balnéo centre offers indoor pools, hydrotherapy, massage and spa treatments for over 18s only (some special family sessions are provided). An inviting outdoor water complex includes two swimming pools, a pool with wave machine, three water slides and a beach area. Competitions and activities include a high season club for children with an entertainer twice a day, a disco once a week and a dance for adults. A member of Leading Campings Group.

You might like to know

You can really get back to nature in one of the tree houses (for 2 to 5 people, no electricity or water) for that true forest experience.

☐ Environmental accreditation
☐ Reduced energy/water consumption policy
☐ Recycling and reusing policy
☑ Information about walking and cycling
☑ Footpaths within 500 m. of the site
☑ Fishing within 1 km.
☐ Riding or pony trekking within 1 km.
☑ Direct river or lake access
☐ Within 10 km. of an area of outstanding natural beauty or national park
☑ Wildlife haven (on site/within 1 km)
☐ Public transport
☑ Dogs welcome

Facilities: Three modern sanitary blocks include some washbasins in cabins and baby bathrooms. Laundry facilities. Facilities for disabled visitors. Motorcaravan services. Shop. Restaurant. Takeaway in bar with terrace. Pool complex. Spa centre. 7-hectare lake (fishing, bathing, canoes, pedaloes). 9-hole golf course. Adventure play area. Tennis. Minigolf. Boules. Roller skating/skateboarding (bring own equipment). Bicycle hire. Internet access and WiFi (charged).

Open: 29 April - 9 September.

Directions: From A71, take Lamotte Beuvron exit (no 3) or from N20 Orléans to Vierzon turn left on to D923 towards Aubigny. After 14 km. turn right at camping sign on to D24E. Site signed in 4 km. GPS: 47.54398, 2.19193

Charges guide

Per unit incl. 2 persons and electricity	€ 20,00 - € 44,00
extra person	€ 7,00 - € 10,00
child (5-17 yrs)	€ 6,00 - € 8,00
child (1-4yrs)	free - € 6,00
dog	€ 5,00 - € 7,00

Kawan Village du Deffay

B.P. 18 Le Deffay, Sainte Reine-de-Bretagne, F-44160 Pontchâteau (Loire-Atlantique)
t: 02 40 88 00 57   e: campingdudeffay@wanadoo.fr
alanrogers.com/FR44090   www.camping-le-deffay.com

Accommodation: ☑Pitch ☑Mobile home/chalet ☑Hotel/B&B ☐ Apartment

A family managed site, Château du Deffay is a refreshing departure from the usual formula in that it is not over organised or supervised and has no tour operator units. The 170 good sized, fairly level pitches have pleasant views and are either on open grass, on shallow terraces divided by hedges, or informally arranged in a central, slightly sloping wooded area. Most have electricity (6/10A). A significant attraction of the site is the large, unfenced lake which is well stocked for fishermen and even has free pedaloes for children. The landscape is wonderfully natural and the site blends well with the rural environment of the estate, lake and farmland which surround it. The bar, restaurant and covered pool are located within the old courtyard area of the smaller château. Alpine type chalets overlook the lake and the larger château, which now offers B&B, provides a wonderful backdrop for an evening stroll. The site is close to the Brière Regional Park, the Guérande Peninsula, and La Baule and is a short drive from the nearest beach.

You might like to know

The nearby Grande Brière national park covers almost 100,000 acres and can be explored by boat. The Guérande salt marshes, a World Heritage Site, produce 12,000 tons of salt every year.

- ☐ Environmental accreditation
- ☑ Reduced energy/water consumption policy
- ☑ Recycling and reusing policy
- ☑ Information about walking and cycling
- ☑ Footpaths within 500 m. of the site
- ☑ Fishing within 1 km.
- ☐ Riding or pony trekking within 1 km.
- ☑ Direct river or lake access
- ☑ Within 10 km. of an area of outstanding natural beauty or national park
- ☑ Wildlife haven (on site/within 1 km)
- ☐ Public transport
- ☑ Dogs welcome

Facilities: The main toilet block is well maintained, if a little dated, and is well equipped including washbasins in cabins, provision for disabled visitors, and a baby bathroom. Laundry facilities. Shop. Bar and small restaurant with takeaway (1/5-15/9). Covered and heated swimming pool (at 28 degrees when we visited) and paddling pool (all season). Play area. TV. Entertainment in season including miniclub. Fishing and pedalos on the lake. Torches useful. WiFi (charged). Off site: Golf 7 km. Riding 10 km. Beach 25 km.

Open: 1 May - 30 September.

Directions: Site is signed from D33 Pontchâteau - Herbignac road near Ste Reine. Also signed from the D773 and N165-E60 (exit 13). GPS: 47.44106, -2.15981

Charges guide

Per unit incl. 2 persons and electricity	€ 18,30 - € 28,20
extra person	€ 3,35 - € 5,60
child (2-12 yrs)	€ 2,30 - € 3,90

Camping les Ajoncs d'Or

Chemin du Rocher, F-44500 La Baule (Loire-Atlantique)
t: 02 40 60 33 29   e: contact@ajoncs.com
alanrogers.com/FR44170   www.ajoncs.com

Accommodation: ☑ Pitch ☑ Mobile home/chalet ☐ Hotel/B&B ☐ Apartment

This site is situated in pine woods, 1.5 km. on the inland side of La Baule and its beautiful bay. A well maintained, natural woodland setting provides a wide variety of pitch types (just over 200), some level and bordered with hedges and tall trees to provide shade and many others that maintain the natural characteristics of the woodland. Most pitches have electricity and water nearby and are usually of a larger size. A central building provides a shop and open friendly bar that serve snacks and takeaways. The new English speaking owner has extensive plans for this campsite. Large areas of woodland have been retained for quiet and recreational purposes and are safe for children to roam. It can be difficult to find an informal campsite close to an exciting seaside resort that retains its touring and camping identity, but Les Ajoncs d'Or does this. Enjoy the gentle breezes off the sea that constantly rustle the trees. The family are justifiably proud of their site.

You might like to know

The salt marshes of the Guérande are a unique sight and can be toured by bicycle.

☐ Environmental accreditation
☑ Reduced energy/water consumption policy
☑ Recycling and reusing policy
☑ Information about walking and cycling
☐ Footpaths within 500 m. of the site
☐ Fishing within 1 km.
☐ Riding or pony trekking within 1 km.
☐ Direct river or lake access
☐ Within 10 km. of an area of outstanding natural beauty or national park
☑ Wildlife haven (on site/within 1 km)
☐ Public transport
☑ Dogs welcome

Facilities: Two good quality sanitary blocks are clean and well maintained providing plenty of facilities including a baby room. Washing machines and dryers. Shop and bar (July/Aug). Snack bar (July/Aug). Good size swimming pool and paddling pool (1/6-5/9). Sports and playground areas. Bicycle hire. Reception with security barrier (closed 22.30-07.30). Off site: Everything for an enjoyable holiday can be found in nearby La Baule. Beach, fishing and riding 1.5 km. Golf 3 km.

Open: 1 April - 30 October.

Directions: From N171 take exit for La Baule les Pins. Follow signs for 'La Baule Centre', then left at roundabout in front of Carrefour supermarket and follow site signs. GPS: 47.28950, -2.37367

Charges guide

Per unit incl. 2 persons and electricity	€ 18,00 - € 30,00
extra person	€ 4,20 - € 7,00
child (2-7 yrs)	€ 2,10 - € 3,50
dog	€ 1,20 - € 2,00

Les Hameaux de Pomette

F-46250 Cazals (Lot)
t: 05 55 84 34 48   e: infos@chalets-en-france.com
alanrogers.com/FR46570   www.chalets-en-france.com/pomette/acc_cazals.html

Accommodation: ☐ Pitch ☑ Mobile home/chalet ☐ Hotel/B&B ☐ Apartment

Les Hameaux de Pomette is an attractive chalet park open all year round. Ideally situated in a lesser known region of France bordered by the departments of the Lot and the Dordogne, it lies in a wooded valley and is a good base for those seeking a quieter holiday in an area known for its culture, nature and gastronomy. The 42 modern chalets are spacious and well equipped with all necessary facilities and have solar panels on the roof to reduce the consumption of electricity. There are three chalets specially adapted for visitors with disabilities. There is a heated swimming pool that can be covered in cooler weather. To the north lies the Dordogne river with its many perched castles and caves famous for their ancient wall paintings. To the south is the valley of the River Lot with its picturesque villages. To the west are the ancient and fortified Bastide towns founded during the 100 years war between England and France. Gourdon, a medieval town 18 km. away, is the nearest large town of interest with its market.

You might like to know

The Lot Valley is a wonderful region of France with some delightful villages, many within easy reach of the campsite.

- ☐ Environmental accreditation
- ☐ Reduced energy/water consumption policy
- ☑ Recycling and reusing policy
- ☑ Information about walking and cycling
- ☑ Footpaths within 500 m. of the site
- ☐ Fishing within 1 km.
- ☐ Riding or pony trekking within 1 km.
- ☐ Direct river or lake access
- ☐ Within 10 km. of an area of outstanding natural beauty or national park
- ☑ Wildlife haven (on site/within 1 km)
- ☐ Public transport
- ☑ Dogs welcome

Facilities: Laundrette. Small shop. Bar. Indoor heated swimming pool. Table tennis. Boules. Play area. TV/games room. Organised activities, excursions and children's club (high season). WiFi at bar and reception (free). Children's cot, iron and linen for hire. Electric barbecues for hire. Off site: Mountain biking. Riding. Tennis. Climbing. Fishing. Canoeing. Minigolf. Nearest small shops, restaurants and Sunday market at Cazals 2 km. Supermarket in Gourdon 18 km.

Open: All year.

Directions: Leave A20 autoroute, exit 51, signed Souillac. Take N20 south, then D673 southwest through Gourdon to Cazals. Take D13 northwest to site (about 3 km). GPS: 44.64948, 1.21688

Charges guide

Contact the site for details.

Kawan Village l'Isle Verte

Avenue de la Loire, F-49730 Montsoreau (Maine-et-Loire)
t: 02 41 51 76 60 e: isleverte@cvtloisirs.fr
alanrogers.com/FR49090 www.campingisleverte.com

Accommodation: ☑Pitch ☑Mobile home/chalet ☐ Hotel/B&B ☐ Apartment

This friendly, natural site, with pitches overlooking the Loire, is just 200 m. from the nearest shop, bar and restaurant in Montsoreau, and is an ideal base from which to explore the western Loire area. Most of the 90 shaded, level and good-sized tourist pitches are separated by low hedges but grass tends to be rather sparse during dry spells. All have electricity (16A). Excellent English is spoken in the reception and bar/restaurant. Attractions within walking distance include the château, troglodyte caves and restaurant, wine tasting in the cellars nearby, and a Sunday market in the town. Fishermen are particularly well catered for at Isle verte, there being an area to store equipment and live bait (permits are available in Saumur). Cyclists and walkers could also well be in their element here. For the less energetic, there is a bus service into Saumur with its château, historic buildings, shops, bars and restaurants. Trains or buses are available in Saumur to take you on to other towns along the Vallée de la Loire.

Special offers
Book for 1 week or more and get a discount of 10% on the ecolodges on stilts (views over the Loire) and fishing lodges made from the site's own recycled trees.

You might like to know
Situated in the Anjou-Touraine nature park, the site is close to vineyards and many places of interest – Fontevraud Abbey and the pretty village of Saumur can be visited by bicycle.

☑ Environmental accreditation
☑ Reduced energy/water consumption policy
☑ Recycling and reusing policy
☑ Information about walking and cycling
☑ Footpaths within 500 m. of the site
☑ Fishing within 1 km.
☐ Riding or pony trekking within 1 km.
☑ Direct river or lake access
☑ Within 10 km. of an area of outstanding natural beauty or national park
☑ Wildlife haven (on site/within 1 km)
☑ Public transport
☑ Dogs welcome

Facilities: A single building provides separate male and female toilets. Washbasins, some in cabins, and showers are unisex. Separate facilities for disabled campers. Baby room. Laundry facilities. Motorcaravan service point. Bar and restaurant (1/5-30/9). Swimming and paddling pools (25/5-30/9). Small play area. Table tennis, volleyball and boules. Fishing. Boat launching. WiFi (charged). Off site: Beach on river 300 m. Bicycle hire and sailing 1 km. Golf and riding both 7 km. 12th-century Abbaye Royale de Fontévraud 5 km. south of Montsoreau.

Open: 1 April - 30 September.

Directions: Montsoreau is 12 km. southeast of Saumur on the D947 towards Chinon. Site is clearly signed on left along the road into town. GPS: 47.21820, 0.05265

Charges guide

Per unit incl. 2 persons and electricity	€ 18,50 - € 22,50
extra person	€ 3,00 - € 4,00
child (5-10 yrs)	€ 2,00 - € 2,50
dog	€ 1,50

Camping l'Etang des Haizes

43 rue Cauticotte, F-50250 Saint Symphorien-le-Valois (Manche)
t: 02 33 46 01 16   e: info@campingetangdeshaizes.com
alanrogers.com/FR50000   www.campingetangdeshaizes.com

Accommodation: ☑Pitch ☑Mobile home/chalet ☐ Hotel/B&B ☐ Apartment

This is an attractive and very friendly site with a swimming pool complex with a four-lane slide, jacuzzi and a paddling pool. L'Etang des Haizes has 160 good size pitches, of which 100 are for touring units, on fairly level ground and all with 10A electricity. They are set in a mixture of conifers, orchard and shrubbery, with some very attractive, slightly smaller pitches overlooking the lake and 60 mobile homes inconspicuously sited. The fenced lake has a small beach (swimming is permitted), with ducks and pedaloes, and offers good coarse fishing for huge carp (we are told!). There are good toilet and shower facilities where children and campers with disabilities are well catered for. Monsieur Laurent, the friendly owner of the site, has recently had an outdoor fitness park installed consisting of eight different pieces of equipment all designed to exercise different parts of the body. This is a good area for walking and cycling and an eight kilometre round trip to experience the views from Le Mont de Doville is a must.

You might like to know
Undergoing accreditation for the rural cycle routes quality charter mark.

☐ Environmental accreditation
☑ Reduced energy/water consumption policy
☑ Recycling and reusing policy
☑ Information about walking and cycling
☑ Footpaths within 500 m. of the site
☑ Fishing within 1 km.
☑ Riding or pony trekking within 1 km.
☑ Direct river or lake access
☑ Within 10 km. of an area of outstanding natural beauty or national park
☑ Wildlife haven (on site/within 1 km)
☑ Public transport
☑ Dogs welcome

Facilities: Two well kept and modern unisex toilet blocks have British style toilets, washbasins in cabins, units for disabled people and two family cabins. Small laundry. Motorcaravan services. Milk, bread and takeaway snacks available (no gas). Snack bar/bar with TV and terrace. Swimming pool complex (all amenities 26/5-2/9). Play areas. Bicycle hire. Pétanque. Organised activities including treasure hunts, archery, water polo and food tasting (5/7-25/8). Tourist information cabin. Wifi (charged). Off site: Riding 1 km. La Haye-du-Puits with 2 supermarkets and restaurants. Beach, Kayaking and Forest Adventure 10 km. Walking and cycle routes.

Open: 1 April - 15 October.

Directions: Site is just north of La Haye-du-Puits on the primary route from Cherbourg to Mont-St-Michel, St Malo and Rennes. It is 24 km. south of N13 at Valognes and 29 km. north of Coutances: leave D900 at roundabout at northern end of bypass (towards town). Site signed on right. GPS: 49.300413, -1.544775

Charges guide

Per unit incl. 2 persons and electricity	€ 16,00 - € 37,00
person (over 4 yrs)	€ 5,00 - € 7,00
dog	€ 1,00 - € 2,00

Yelloh! Village Le Domaine d'Inly

Route de Couarne, B.P. 24, F-56760 Pénestin-sur-Mer (Morbihan)
t: 02 99 90 35 09 e: inly-info@wanadoo.fr
alanrogers.com/FR56240 www.camping-inly.com

Accommodation: ☑Pitch ☑Mobile home/chalet ☐ Hotel/B&B ☐ Apartment

This very large site is mainly taken up with mobile homes and cottages, some belonging to the site owner, some private and some belonging to tour operators. Most of these pitches are arranged in groups of 10 to 14 around a central stone circle with a water point in the middle. Of the 500 pitches, 80 are for touring units and all are large (150-200 sq.m) with a 10A electrical connection (Europlug). Most are level and are situated by the attractive lake at the bottom of the site where one can fish or canoe. Pony rides are possible around the lake. The heated swimming pool, with its slides, and the bar and restaurant area, form two sides of an attractive courtyard. You will enjoy the indoor swimming pool which is open every day of the season, as well as a beauty area and a variety of sporting and leisure activities.

You might like to know

Pénestin, a typically Breton small town, is near 25 km. of coastline and has a pretty beach at La Mine d'Or.

- ☐ Environmental accreditation
- ☐ Reduced energy/water consumption policy
- ☑ Recycling and reusing policy
- ☑ Information about walking and cycling
- ☑ Footpaths within 500 m. of the site
- ☑ Fishing within 1 km.
- ☐ Riding or pony trekking within 1 km.
- ☐ Direct river or lake access
- ☐ Within 10 km. of an area of outstanding natural beauty or national park
- ☑ Wildlife haven (on site/within 1 km)
- ☐ Public transport
- ☑ Dogs welcome

Facilities: One toilet block (an additional block is planned) with facilities for disabled visitors, and a baby room. Laundry. Shop. Small, comfortable bar with large screen satellite TV, attractive restaurant and takeaway (all season). Heated swimming pool complex with slide (outdoor 15/5-15/9, indoor all season). Games room. Play areas. Football pitch (weekly games organised in July/Aug). Wellness (all season). Lake for fishing/canoeing. Bicycle hire. WiFi. Off site: Supermarket 1 km. Pénestin town centre 2 km. Beach 2 km. Sailing and boat launching 2.5 km. Riding 15 km. Golf 25 km.

Open: 6 April - 22 September.

Directions: From D34 from La Roche-Bernard, at roundabout just after entering Pénestin take D201 south, signed Assérac. After 100 m. take first turning on left (site signed) opposite Carrefour supermarket. After 650 m. turn right, again signed, and campsite is 400 m. on left. GPS: 47.471483, -2.467267

Charges guide

Per unit incl. 2 persons and electricity	€ 17,00 - € 42,00
extra person	€ 6,00 - € 7,00
child (3-7 yrs)	free - € 6,00
dog	€ 4,00

Camping le Bois du Valmarie

F-66702 Argelès-sur-Mer (Pyrénées-Orientales)

t: 04 68 81 09 92   e: contact@camping-lasirene.fr

alanrogers.com/FR66590   www.camping-lasirene.fr

Accommodation: ☐ Pitch   ☑ Mobile home/chalet   ☐ Hotel/B&B   ☐ Apartment

Pitches here are exclusively for mobile home and chalet accommodation. Le Bois du Valmarie is a member of the same group of sites as La Sirène and L'Hippocampe. The site has 181 pitches, the majority of which are available for booking (none available for touring) and is located south of the port beside Racou beach. The site has a pleasant woodland location and a range of amenities including a large swimming pool complex with waterslides and a separate children's pool. The sea is just 50 m. from the site entrance with a sandy beach and within easy walking distance. The site has its own bar and a good restaurant but visitors are welcome at La Sirene to enjoy the entertainment and activities on offer. The site is popular with tour operators.

You might like to know

The campsite is on the Racou beach, 7 km. of glorious sands overlooked by watch towers, perfectly situated between the mountains and the sea.

☐ Environmental accreditation
☑ Reduced energy/water consumption policy
☑ Recycling and reusing policy
☑ Information about walking and cycling
☑ Footpaths within 500 m. of the site
☑ Fishing within 1 km.
☐ Riding or pony trekking within 1 km.
☐ Direct river or lake access
☑ Within 10 km. of an area of outstanding natural beauty or national park
☑ Wildlife haven (on site/within 1 km)
☑ Public transport
☑ Dogs welcome

Facilities: Supermarket. Restaurant. Bar. Beach shop. Takeaway food. Swimming pool with waterslides and separate children's pool. Play area. Mobile homes for rent. Off site: Argelès town centre 3 km. Diving club. Blue Bear activity club. Emeraude Beach Club. Fishing 2 km. Riding 4 km. Golf 7 km.

Open: 7 April - 28 September.

Directions: Leave autoroute at Perpignan-Sud exit and join the N114 southbound toward Argelès. Take exit 13 and follow signs to Le Racou. Site is well signed from here. GPS: 42.53784, 3.05445

Charges guide

Contact the site for details.

Camping les Lanchettes

F-73210 Peisey-Nancroix (Savoie)
t: 04 79 07 93 07   e: lanchettes@free.fr
alanrogers.com/FR73030   www.camping-lanchettes.com

Accommodation: ☑ Pitch ☑ Mobile home/chalet ☐ Hotel/B&B ☐ Apartment

This site is close to the beautiful Vanoise National Park and at 1,470 m. is one of the highest campsites in this guide. There is a steep climb to the site but the spectacular scenery is well worth the effort. It is a natural, terraced site with 90 good size, reasonably level and well drained, grassy/stony pitches, with 70 used for touring units, all having electricity (3-10A). Outside taps are only available in summer because of the altitude and cold winters. For those who love walking and biking, wonderful scenery, flora and fauna, this is the site for you. Underpowered units are not advised to attempt the climb. In winter it is ideal for the serious skier being close to the famous resort of Les Arcs (via free bus service and cable car) and about 30 of the pitches at the bottom of the site are unused as they become part of a cross country ski run. A wide range of footpaths and mountain bike rides are available in the valley and mountains around.

Special offers

10% reduction on the entry price to the adventure park, just 100 m. from the campsite.

You might like to know

A shuttle bus stops at the site entrance to take you to the 425 km. of ski slopes. There is also direct access to a further 42 km. of slopes.

☐ Environmental accreditation
☐ Reduced energy/water consumption policy
☑ Recycling and reusing policy
☑ Information about walking and cycling
☑ Footpaths within 500 m. of the site
☑ Fishing within 1 km.
☐ Riding or pony trekking within 1 km.
☑ Direct river or lake access
☐ Within 10 km. of an area of outstanding natural beauty or national park
☑ Wildlife haven (on site/within 1 km)
☐ Public transport
☑ Dogs welcome

Facilities: Well appointed heated toilet block. Motorcaravan services. Restaurant, takeaway (July/Aug. and winter). Playground. Club/TV room. Large tent/marquee used in bad weather. In winter a small bus (free) runs to the ski lifts every 30 minutes. Free WiFi. Off site: Riding next to site. Peisey-Nancroix, restaurants, bars and shops 3 km. Les Arcs winter sports centre, outdoor swimming pool and bicycle hire 6 km. Golf and indoor pool 8 km. Lakeside beach 10 km. Walks in National Park.

Open: 15 December - 30 April, 1 June - 15 October.

Directions: From Albertville take N90 towards Bourg-St-Maurice, through Aime. In 9 km. turn right on D87, signed Peisey-Nancroix. Follow a winding hilly road (with hairpin bends) for 10 km. Pass through Peisey-Nancroix; site on right about 1 km. beyond Nancroix. GPS: 45.53137, 6.77560

Charges guide

Per unit incl. 2 persons and electricity	€ 12,50 - € 14,10
extra person	€ 4,20 - € 4,70
child (2-7 yrs)	€ 2,30 - € 2,55
dog	€ 1,30 - € 1,60

Camping les Dômes de Miage

197 route des Contamines, F-74170 Saint Gervais-les-Bains (Haute-Savoie)
t: 04 50 93 45 96 e: info@camping-mont-blanc.com
alanrogers.com/FR74140 www.camping-mont-blanc.com

Accommodation: ☑ Pitch ☑ Mobile home/chalet ☐ Hotel/B&B ☐ Apartment

Saint Gervais is a pretty spa town in the picturesque Val-Monjoie valley and this site is 2 km. from its centre. It is 22 km. west of Chamonix and centrally located for discovering this marvellous mountain region. Nestled among the mountains, this sheltered, well equipped site provides 150 flat grassy pitches. Of a good size, about half have shade and there are 100 with electricity points (3-10A). The remainder on terraced ground are used for tents. Third generation hosts, Stéphane and Sophie, will welcome you to the site and their passion for this area at the foot of Mont Blanc is infectious. A number of Savoyard style chalets to let are planned for the future. This is a good site for large motorcaravans. There is no on-site entertainment programme, but a wealth of information about the area and activities available nearby is provided at reception where they will help you plan your itinerary. There is a bus service into Saint Gervais, from where there is a frequent shuttle bus to its spa and a tramway to the Mont Blanc range.

You might like to know

The site is located at the foot of Mont Blanc in a natural setting. The Alpine animal park (Merlet in Les Houches) and natural reserves (Les Contamines Montjoie, Les Aiguilles Rouges Chamonix) are within easy reach.

☑ Environmental accreditation
☑ Reduced energy/water consumption policy
☑ Recycling and reusing policy
☑ Information about walking and cycling
☑ Footpaths within 500 m. of the site
☑ Fishing within 1 km.
☐ Riding or pony trekking within 1 km.
☐ Direct river or lake access
☑ Within 10 km. of an area of outstanding natural beauty or national park
☑ Wildlife haven (on site/within 1 km)
☑ Public transport
☑ Dogs welcome

Facilities: Two sanitary blocks, one heated, with a suite for disabled visitors and baby room. Washing machines, dryer. Motorcaravan services. Small basic shop. Bar/restaurant. TV room, library, ironing board. Excellent playground. Playing field. Off site: Fishing 100 m. Bicycle hire 1 km. Riding 7 km. Shops, etc. and outdoor swimming pool in St Gervais.

Open: 1 May - 12 September.

Directions: From St Gervais take D902 towards Les Contamines and site is on left after 2 km. GPS: 45.87389, 6.7199

Charges guide

Per unit incl. 2 persons and electricity	€ 20,10 - € 26,10
extra person	€ 3,00 - € 4,10
child (2-9 yrs)	€ 2,50 - € 3,50
dog	free - € 2,00

Camping le Clos Cacheleux

Route de Bouillancourt, F-80132 Miannay (Somme)
t: 03 22 19 17 47   e: raphael@camping-lecloscacheleux.fr
alanrogers.com/FR80210   www.camping-lecloscacheleux.fr

Accommodation: ☑ Pitch ☑ Mobile home/chalet ☐ Hotel/B&B ☐ Apartment

Le Clos Cacheleux is a well situated campsite of six hectares bordering woodland in the park of the Château Bouillancourt which dates from the 18th century. The site was first opened in July 2008. It is 11 km. from the Bay of the Somme, regarded as being amongst the most beautiful bays in France. There are 100 very large, grassy pitches (200 sq.m) and all have electricity hook-ups and water points. The aim of the owners is to make your stay as enjoyable as possible by providing high quality services and activities. Visitors have access to the swimming pool, bar and children's club of the sister site – Le Val de Trie (20 m). During high season fresh bread and croissants are delivered to your pitch. There is a children's farm with rabbits, sheep, goats, cows and hens. Ask at reception for free walking and cycling tours. A Sites et Paysages member.

You might like to know

The campsite is situated in the grounds of a magnificent 18th-century castle.

☐ Environmental accreditation
☐ Reduced energy/water consumption policy
☑ Recycling and reusing policy
☑ Information about walking and cycling
☑ Footpaths within 500 m. of the site
☐ Fishing within 1 km.
☑ Riding or pony trekking within 1 km.
☐ Direct river or lake access
☐ Within 10 km. of an area of outstanding natural beauty or national park
☑ Wildlife haven (on site/within 1 km)
☐ Public transport
☐ Dogs welcome

Facilities: The single sanitary block is clean and well maintained. Facilities for disabled visitors. Baby room. Laundry room with washing machine and dryer. Motorcaravan service point. At the sister site: shop (all season), bar with terrace (1/4-15/10), library and TV room, restaurant and takeaway (26/4-4/9). Play area. Boules. Picnic tables. Freezer for ice packs. Barbecue hire. Bicycle hire. Fishing pond. Caravan storage. There is also a covered pool (15/4-30/9) on the sister site and a second sanitary block with family showers plus children's facilities. Off site: Village 1 km. Hypermarket in Abbéville. Riding 4 km. Golf 9 km. Sandy beaches of the Picardy coast 12 km.

Open: 15 March - 15 October.

Directions: From the A28 at Abbéville take the D925 towards Eu and Le Tréport; do not go towards Moyenville. Turn left in Miannay village on the D86 towards Toeufles. The road to Bouillancourt-sous-Miannay is on the left after 2 km. and site is signed in the village. GPS: 50.08352, 1.71343

Charges guide

Per unit incl. 2 persons and electricity	€ 18,50 - € 25,80
extra person	€ 3,10 - € 5,30
child (under 7 yrs)	€ 1,90 - € 3,30

Les Hameaux des Lacs

F-82230 Monclar de Quercy (Tarn-et-Garonne)
t: 05 55 84 34 48 e: info@chalets-en-france.com
alanrogers.com/FR82060 www.chalets-en-france.com

Accommodation: ☐ Pitch ☑ Mobile home/chalet ☐ Hotel/B&B ☐ Apartment

Les Hameaux des Lacs is a member of the Chalets en France group. This group comprises six chalet parks in southern France. Please note, however, that there are no touring pitches here. The site is open all year and can be found at the heart of the Tarn et Garonne department, south east of Montauban and forms part of a 'base de loisirs'. Leisure facilities on offer here include tennis, an equestrian centre, a swimming pool, and a multisports pitch. Sailing and windsurfing are popular on the lake, and fishing is also possible. Chalets here are attractively dispersed around the site and are all available for rent. During the summer months, the entertainment makes use of the lake and swimming pools but it should be noted that the swimming complex is only open from May to October. A comprehensive entertainment programme designed to suit ages from 4 to 12 is provided. There are visiting horses for young children (once per week) and a regular train around the lake for old and young alike. A reflexologist visits weekly.

You might like to know

Great fun can be had on the many lakes surrounding the site, which are a focal point of the beautiful landscape.

- ☑ Environmental accreditation
- ☑ Reduced energy/water consumption policy
- ☑ Recycling and reusing policy
- ☑ Information about walking and cycling
- ☑ Footpaths within 500 m. of the site
- ☑ Fishing within 1 km.
- ☑ Riding or pony trekking within 1 km.
- ☐ Direct river or lake access
- ☐ Within 10 km. of an area of outstanding natural beauty or national park
- ☑ Wildlife haven (on site/within 1 km)
- ☐ Public transport
- ☑ Dogs welcome

Facilities: Swimming pool (15/5-30/9). Play area. Children's club. Multisport pitch. Games room. Tourist information. Entertainment and activity programme. WiFi. Chalets for rent. Off site: Base de Loisirs with swimming pool. Lake with beach. Sailing and windsurfing. Fishing. Riding centre. Cycle and walking trails.

Open: All year.

Directions: Take exit 61 from the A20 motorway (Montauban) and then head east on the D8 to Montclar de Quercy. The site is well signed at Base de Loisirs upon arrival in the town. GPS: 43.96565, 1.58469

Charges guide

Contact the site for details.

FRANCE – Bormes-les-Mimosas

Camp du Domaine

B.P. 207 La Favière, F-83230 Bormes-les-Mimosas (Var)
t: 04 94 71 03 12 e: mail@campdudomaine.com
alanrogers.com/FR83120 www.campdudomaine.com

Accommodation: ☑Pitch ☑Mobile home/chalet ☐Hotel/B&B ☐Apartment

Camp du Domaine, 3 km. south of Le Lavandou, is a large, attractive beachside site with 1,200 pitches set in 45 hectares of pinewood, although surprisingly it does not give the impression of being so big. The pitches are large (up to 200 sq.m) and most are reasonably level, 800 with 10A electricity. The most popular pitches are beside the beach, but the ones furthest away are generally larger and have more shade. Amongst the trees, many are more suitable for tents. The price for all the pitches is the same – smaller but near the beach or larger with shade. The beach is the attraction and everyone tries to get close. American motorhomes are not accepted. Despite its size, the site does not feel too busy, except perhaps around the supermarket. This is mainly because many pitches are hidden in the trees, the access roads are quite wide and it all covers quite a large area (some of the beach pitches are 600 m. from the entrance). Its popularity makes early reservation necessary over a long season.

Special offers
50% reduction on the second week for 5 people booking a bungalow or mobile home. Best reductions are in May and June.

You might like to know
The campsite is located near the sea and has typical Mediterranean vegetation. There are boats from Lavandou Harbour (3 km) to Port Cros Islands, a popular tourist destination.

☐ Environmental accreditation
☑ Reduced energy/water consumption policy
☑ Recycling and reusing policy
☑ Information about walking and cycling
☑ Footpaths within 500 m. of the site
☐ Fishing within 1 km.
☐ Riding or pony trekking within 1 km.
☐ Direct river or lake access
☑ Within 10 km. of an area of outstanding natural beauty or national park
☐ Wildlife haven (on site/within 1 km)
☑ Public transport
☐ Dogs welcome

Facilities: Ten modern, well used but clean toilet blocks. Mostly Turkish WCs. Facilities for disabled visitors (but steep steps). Baby room. Washing machines. Fridge hire. Well stocked supermarket, bars, pizzeria (all open all season). No swimming pool. Excellent play area. Boats, pedalos for hire. Wide range of watersports. Games, competitions (July/Aug). Children's club. Tennis. Multisport courts. Barbecues are strictly forbidden. Dogs are not accepted 10/7-21/8. Off site: Bicycle hire 500 m. Riding and golf 15 km.

Open: 9 April - 5 November.

Directions: From Bormes-les Mimosas, head east on D559 to Le Lavandou. At roundabout, turn off D559 towards the sea on road signed Favière. After 2 km. turn left at site signs. GPS: 43.11779, 6.35176

Charges guide

Per unit incl. 2 persons and electricity	€ 28,50 - € 43,00
extra person	€ 6,00 - € 9,50
child (under 7 yrs)	€ 1,00 - € 4,80
dog (not 10/7-21/8)	free

Camping les Lacs du Verdon

Domaine de Roquelande, F-83630 Régusse (Var)
t: 04 94 70 17 95 e: info@lacs-verdon.com
alanrogers.com/FR83140 www.leslacsduverdon.com

Accommodation: ☑ Pitch ☑ Mobile home/chalet ☐ Hotel/B&B ☐ Apartment

In beautiful countryside and within easy reach of the Grand Canyon du Verdon and its nearby lakes, this site is only 90 minutes from Cannes. It is now part of the Homair Vacances chain and is currently run by Christophe Laurent and his team who are immensely proud of their site and the high standard they have achieved. The 30 acre wooded park is divided in two by a minor road. The 480 very stony, but level pitches (rock pegs advised) are marked and separated by stones and trees. Of these, 107 are available for tourists, many an irregular shape, but all are of average size with electricity (long leads may be necessary). The part across the road is used mainly for mobile homes but has some pitches for tourers, ideal for those wanting peace and quiet away from the main area. The site is very attractive, clean and well cared for and is most suitable for families with almost all facilities open from the beginning of the season. A lovely restaurant and bar area serves breakfast, lunch and dinner.

You might like to know

There is plenty to do on site: children's club, playgrounds, tennis, minigolf, swimming pool, as well as a bar, restaurant and shop. If you want to venture further afield, there are many places of interest locally, notably the Gorges du Verdon (15 km).

☐ Environmental accreditation
☑ Reduced energy/water consumption policy
☑ Recycling and reusing policy
☑ Information about walking and cycling
☐ Footpaths within 500 m. of the site
☐ Fishing within 1 km.
☑ Riding or pony trekking within 1 km.
☐ Direct river or lake access
☑ Within 10 km. of an area of outstanding natural beauty or national park
☑ Wildlife haven (on site/within 1 km)
☐ Public transport
☑ Dogs welcome

Facilities: Modernised toilet blocks have mainly British style WCs and some washbasins in cubicles. Laundry and dishwashing facilities. Small supermarket. Bar. Restaurant and pizzeria. Attractive and heated swimming pool/paddling pool complex. Artificial grass tennis courts. Minigolf. Outdoor exercise equipment. Boules. Bicycle hire. Playground. TV and teenage games room. Entertainment programme. Discos, dances and theme nights. Only electric barbecues are permitted. WiFi (charged). Off site: Régusse 2.5 km. Aups 7 km. Riding 10 km. Fishing, beach, sailing and windsurfing at Saint Croix 15 km.

Open: 29 April - 23 September.

Directions: Leave A8 motorway at St Maximin and take D560 northeast (Barjols). At Barjols turn left on D71 (Montmeyan), turn right on D30 (Régusse) and follow site signs. GPS: 43.6602, 6.1511

Charges guide

Per unit incl. 1 or 2 persons and 16A electricity	€ 15,00 - € 26,00
extra person	€ 3,00 - € 5,50
child (3-6 yrs)	free - € 4,50
dog	€ 1,50

Camping la Yole

Chemin des Bosses, Orouet, F-85160 Saint Jean-de-Monts (Vendée)
t: 02 51 58 67 17 e: contact@la-yole.com
alanrogers.com/FR85150 www.la-yole.com

Accommodation: ☑ Pitch ☑ Mobile home/chalet ☐ Hotel/B&B ☐ Apartment

La Yole is an attractive and well run site, two kilometres from a sandy beach. It offers 369 pitches, some of which are occupied by tour operators and mobile homes to rent. There are 180 touring pitches, most with shade and separated by bushes and trees. A newer area at the rear of the site is a little more open. All the pitches are of at least 100 sq.m. and have electricity (10A), water and drainage. The pool complex includes an attractive outdoor pool, a paddling pool, slide and an indoor heated pool with jacuzzi. There are also new gym facilities. Entertainment is organised in high season. This is a clean and tidy site, ideal for families with children and you will receive a helpful and friendly welcome.

You might like to know

Just a few metres from the site there are numerous flat cycle paths and the forest of St Jean-de-Monts. Nestling in a natural area between fields and woodland, there are some outstanding places to visit – Noirmoutier, the Ile d'Yeu, Puy du Fou.

☐ Environmental accreditation
☑ Reduced energy/water consumption policy
☑ Recycling and reusing policy
☑ Information about walking and cycling
☑ Footpaths within 500 m. of the site
☐ Fishing within 1 km.
☑ Riding or pony trekking within 1 km.
☐ Direct river or lake access
☑ Within 10 km. of an area of outstanding natural beauty or national park
☐ Wildlife haven (on site/within 1 km)
☐ Public transport
☑ Dogs welcome

Facilities: Two toilet blocks include washbasins in cabins and facilities for disabled visitors and babies. A third block has a baby room. Laundry facilities. Shop (15/5-5/9). Bar, restaurant and takeaway (1/5-15/9). Outdoor pool and paddling pool. Indoor heated pool with jacuzzi (all season, no shorts). Gym centre. Play area. Club room. Tennis. Games room. Entertainment in high season. WiFi (charged). Gas barbecues only. Max. 1 dog. Off site: Beach, bus service, bicycle hire 2 km. Riding 3 km. Fishing, golf and watersports 6 km.

Open: 2 April - 21 September.

Directions: Site is signed off the D38, 6 km. south of St Jean-de-Monts in the village of Orouet. Coming from St Jean-de-Monts turn right at l'Oasis restaurant towards Mouette and follow signs to site. GPS: 46.75659, -2.00792

Charges guide

Per unit incl. 2 persons and electricity	€ 16,00 - € 31,00
extra person	€ 3,70 - € 6,80
child (under 9 yrs)	free - € 5,50
dog	€ 4,00 - € 5,00

Camping Domaine de la Forêt

Route de Martinet, F-85150 Saint Julien-des-Landes (Vendée)
t: 02 51 46 62 11 e: camping@domainelaforet.com
alanrogers.com/FR85820 www.domainelaforet.com

Accommodation: ☑Pitch ☑Mobile home/chalet ☐ Hotel/B&B ☐ Apartment

Set in the tranquil and beautiful natural parkland surrounding an 18th-century château, this lovely site has 200 large pitches, of which 167 are for touring units. There are five units for rent and 28 pitches are occupied by tour operators. All are on grass and fully serviced including 6A electricity; some are in shady woodland and others, for sun worshippers, are more open. The camping area is only a small part of the 50-hectare estate, with a mix of woodland, open meadows and fishing lakes, all accessible to campers. The many outbuildings around the courtyard have been tastefully converted and include a bar and restaurant in the old stables. There are two outdoor swimming pools, one on each side of the château. Children will have a great time here exploring the vast, unrestricted area and sometimes hidden corners of this site in Swallows and Amazons style. However, parents should note there are open, unfenced fishing lakes and barns with tractors and machinery.

You might like to know

The nearest beach is just 12 km. away and easily reached by car. Closer to the site, there is karting for the children, and museums for adults.

- ☐ Environmental accreditation
- ☐ Reduced energy/water consumption policy
- ☐ Recycling and reusing policy
- ☑ Information about walking and cycling
- ☐ Footpaths within 500 m. of the site
- ☑ Fishing within 1 km.
- ☑ Riding or pony trekking within 1 km.
- ☐ Direct river or lake access
- ☐ Within 10 km. of an area of outstanding natural beauty or national park
- ☑ Wildlife haven (on site/within 1 km)
- ☐ Public transport
- ☑ Dogs welcome

Facilities: Two large good quality sanitary blocks include washbasins in cubicles, with good provision for babies and disabled campers. Laundry facilities with washing machines and dryers. Bar/restaurant with TV. Two heated outdoor swimming pools (one for children with slide, one for serious swimmers). Regular evening entertainment, children's clubs and disco (July/Aug). Adventure playground, trampoline and games room. Tennis. Boules. Fishing lakes. 6-hole swing golf course (pitch and putt with soft balls) and minigolf. Canoeing trips. WiFi. Only gas barbecues permitted. No double axle caravans accepted. Off site: Equestrian centre, bicycle hire 200 m. ATM at La Mothe-Achard 5 km. Golf and beaches 12 km.

Open: 15 May - 15 September.

Directions: St Julien-des-Landes is 25 km. west of La Roche-sur-Yon, northwest of La Mothe-Achard. From La Mothe-Achard take the D12 to St Julien, turn northeast on D55 at crossroads towards Martinet. The site is on left almost immediately (signed). GPS: 46.6432, -1.71198

Charges guide

Per unit incl. 2 persons and electricity	€ 17,70 - € 33,20
extra person	€ 3,10 - € 6,30
child (2-17 yrs)	€ 3,10 - € 6,00

Camping Domaine des Messires

1 rue des Messires, F-88600 Herpelmont (Vosges)
t: 03 29 58 56 29 e: mail@domainedesmessires.com
alanrogers.com/FR88070 www.domainedesmessires.com

Accommodation: ☑Pitch ☑Mobile home/chalet ☐ Hotel/B&B ☐ Apartment

Nestling in woods beside a lake, des Messires is a haven of peace and perfect for nature lovers – not just birds and flowers but beavers, too. The Vosges is famous for its mountains and you can easily cross the Col de Schlucht to the Moselle vineyards and the medieval villages like Riquewihr with their old walls and storks on chimneys. The 110 good sized and fully serviced pitches are on grass over stone, with some directly by the lakeside, excellent for fishing. When the day is over, enjoy a leisurely meal at the restaurant overlooking the lake or just relax over a glass of wine. There are also 22 mobile homes for rent. For the more active, canoes are available free of charge in low season; swim in the lake or visit the nearby partner site for a swim in their pool. Should the weather be inclement, try some of the old-fashioned wooden games, play indoor minigolf or watch the satellite TV in the lounge with its open fire, near the bar. You are going to be spoilt for choice. Groups are catered for away from the main touring section.

Special offers
In low season stay 7 nights, pay for 6 and stay 14 nights, pay for 11.

You might like to know
This is a beautiful wooded site where you will be welcomed not only by the birds on site but the beavers too!

☐ Environmental accreditation
☐ Reduced energy/water consumption policy
☐ Recycling and reusing policy
☑ Information about walking and cycling
☑ Footpaths within 500 m. of the site
☑ Fishing within 1 km.
☐ Riding or pony trekking within 1 km.
☑ Direct river or lake access
☑ Within 10 km. of an area of outstanding natural beauty or national park
☑ Wildlife haven (on site/within 1 km)
☐ Public transport
☑ Dogs welcome

Facilities: The fully equipped, modern, airy toilet block includes all washbasins in cabins, provision for disabled visitors (key from reception), baby room and laundry. Bar and restaurant overlooking the lake (both 1/5-1/10). Takeaway (1/5-1/10). Two small play areas. Games and TV room. Canoeing and lake swimming. Programme of activities for children and adults in high season. WiFi (charged). Off site: Weekly markets in nearby Bruyères, Corcieux and St Dié. Riding and golf 12 km.

Open: 23 April - 18 September.

Directions: From Épinal, exit N57 on N420 for St Dié and follow signs until you pick up signs for Bruyères. Lac du Messires is signed as you leave Bruyères on D423, at Laveline go south to Herpelmont and site. GPS: 48.1787, 6.74309

Charges guide

Per unit incl. 2 persons and electricity	€ 18,00 - € 26,00
extra person	€ 4,00 - € 6,50
child (6-12 yrs)	€ 3,00 - € 5,00
dog	€ 3,00 - € 4,00

South Penquite Farm

South Penquite, Blisland, Bodmin PL30 4LH (Cornwall)
t: 01208 850491 e: thefarm@bodminmoor.co.uk
alanrogers.com/UK0302 www.southpenquite.co.uk

Accommodation: ☑Pitch ☑Mobile home/chalet ☐ Hotel/B&B ☐ Apartment

South Penquite offers real camping with no frills, set on a 200 hectare hill farm high on Bodmin Moor between the villages of Blisland and St Breward. The farm achieved organic status in 2001 and runs a flock of 300 ewes and a herd of 40 cattle and horses. The camping is small scale and intended to have a low impact on the surrounding environment. Fifty tents or simple motorcaravans (no caravans) can pitch around the edge of three walled fields, roughly cut in the midst of the moor. You can find shelter or a view. Four Yurts – round Mongolian tents – are available to rent in one field, complete with wood burning stoves – quite original. Camp fires are permitted with wood available from the farmhouse. You will also find horses, ponies, chickens, geese, ducks and turkeys which show their approval (or not) by the skin around their necks changing colour! A walk of some two miles takes you over most of the farm and some of the moor, taking in a Bronze Age hut settlement, the river and a standing stone.

You might like to know

There are opportunities to study a variety of subjects from butterflies to archaeology!

☐ Environmental accreditation
☑ Reduced energy/water consumption policy
☑ Recycling and reusing policy
☑ Information about walking and cycling
☑ Footpaths within 500 m. of the site
☑ Fishing within 1 km.
☑ Riding or pony trekking within 1 km.
☑ Direct river or lake access
☐ Within 10 km. of an area of outstanding natural beauty or national park
☑ Wildlife haven (on site/within 1 km)
☐ Public transport
☐ Dogs welcome

Facilities: A smart new pine clad toilet block, with a separate provision of four family-sized showers, with solar heated rainwater. Two covered dishwashing sinks (H&C) and two outside sinks. Washing machine and dryer. Small fridge and freezer. Home produced lamb, burgers and sausages. LPG gas. Facilities for field studies, and for educational groups and schools to learn about the local environment. Bushcraft days. Fishing (requires an EA rod licence). Dogs are not accepted. Off site: Walking. Riding and cycling 1 mile. Pubs 1.5 and 2.5 miles. Sustrans Route 3 passes close by.

Open: 1 May - 1 November.

Directions: On the A30 over Bodmin Moor pass Jamaica Inn and sign for Colliford Lake and watch for St Breward sign (to right) immediately at end of dual-carriageway. Follow this narrow road over open moor for 2 miles ignoring any turns to left or right. Also ignore right turn to St Breward just before the South Penquite sign. Follow track over stone bridge beside ford through farm gate and then bear to left to camping fields. Walk back to book in at Farm House. GPS: 50.5445, -4.671833

Charges guide

Per person	£ 7,00
child (5-16 yrs)	£ 3,50

Hidden Valley Touring Park

West Down, Ilfracombe EX34 8NU (Devon)
t: **01271 813837** e: relax@hiddenvalleypark.com
alanrogers.com/UK0710 www.hiddenvalleypark.com

Accommodation: ☑Pitch ☐ Mobile home/chalet ☐ Hotel/B&B ☐ Apartment

The owners, the Legg family, run this aptly named family park to high standards. In a sheltered valley setting between Barnstaple and Ilfracombe beside a small stream and lake (with ducks), it is most attractive and is also convenient for several resorts, beaches and the surrounding countryside. The original part of the park offers some 67 level pitches on three sheltered terraces. On hardstanding, all have electricity (16A) and TV connections (leads for hire), with a water point between each pitch. Kingfisher Meadow, a little way from the main facilities and reached by a tarmac road, provides a further 58 pitches. These are entirely on grass (so suitable for campers with tents) and all have electricity, water, drain and TV hook-up. Two good adventure play areas have wooden equipment (one near a fast flowing stream which is fenced). Essentially this is a park for those seeking good quality facilities in very attractive, natural surroundings, without too many man-made distractions – apart from some traffic noise during the daytime.

You might like to know

The Hidden Valley Touring and Camping Park has received a number of awards and is popular with nature lovers, who have spotted kingfishers, otters, deer and buzzards.

☐ Environmental accreditation
☐ Reduced energy/water consumption policy
☑ Recycling and reusing policy
☑ Information about walking and cycling
☑ Footpaths within 500 m. of the site
☐ Fishing within 1 km.
☐ Riding or pony trekking within 1 km.
☐ Direct river or lake access
☐ Within 10 km. of an area of outstanding natural beauty or national park
☑ Wildlife haven (on site/within 1 km)
☐ Public transport
☑ Dogs welcome

Facilities: Two modern heated toilet blocks are tiled and have non-slip floors. Some washbasins in cubicles, some en-suite with toilets in the Kingfisher Meadow block. Bathroom. Baby room. Complete facilities for visitors with disabilities. Laundry facilities. Motorcaravan service facilities. Gas supplies. Shop. Coffee shop serving breakfast and light lunches. Play areas. Dogs exercise area. Caravan storage. Off site: Fishing and golf 2 miles. Bicycle hire 4 miles. Beach 4.5 miles. Riding 5 miles.

Open: All year.

Directions: Park is on the A361 Barnstaple - Ilfracombe road, 3.5 miles after Braunton. GPS: 51.146533, -4.14555

Charges guide

Per unit incl. 2 persons	£ 15,00 - £ 40,00
extra person	£ 3,00 - £ 5,00
child (2-15 yrs)	free - £ 4,00
dog	£ 1,50

 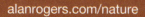

Kelling Heath Holiday Park

Weybourne, Holt, Sheringham NR25 7HW (Norfolk)
t: **01263 588181**   e: info@kellingheath.co.uk
alanrogers.com/UK3430   www.kellingheath.co.uk

Accommodation: ☑ Pitch ☑ Mobile home/chalet ☐ Hotel/B&B ☐ Apartment

Not many parks can boast their own railway station and Kelling Heath's own halt on the North Norfolk Steam Railway gives access to the beach at Sheringham. Set in 250 acres of woodland and heathland, this very spacious holiday park offers freedom and relaxation with 300 large, level, grass touring pitches, all with 16A electricity and six are fully serviced. Together with 384 caravan holiday homes (36 to let, the rest privately owned), they blend easily into the part-wooded, part-open heath. A wide range of facilities provides activities for all ages. 'The Forge' has an entertainment bar and a family room, with comprehensive entertainment all season. The leisure centre provides an indoor pool, spa pool, sauna, steam rooms and gym. The central reception area is attractively paved to provide a village square with an open air bandstand. The park's natural environment allows for woodland walks, a nature trail and cycling trails, and a small lake for fishing (permit holders only).

Special offers
Special offers are often available.
Visit www.kellingheath.co.uk for details.

You might like to know
Set amongst rare open heathland with backdrops of pine and native woodland. A magnificent range of facilities and environmental activities are offered for the whole family.

☑ Environmental accreditation
☑ Reduced energy/water consumption policy
☑ Recycling and reusing policy
☑ Information about walking and cycling
☑ Footpaths within 500 m. of the site
☑ Fishing within 1 km.
☑ Riding or pony trekking within 1 km.
☐ Direct river or lake access
☑ Within 10 km. of an area of outstanding natural beauty or national park
☑ Wildlife haven (on site/within 1 km)
☑ Public transport
☑ Dogs welcome

Facilities: Three toilet blocks include facilities for disabled visitors, a baby room and dishwashing and laundry sinks. Laundry facilities. Well stocked shop. Gas. Bar, restaurant and takeaway (all season). Indoor leisure centre with pool, gym, etc. with trained staff (membership on either daily or weekly basis). Outdoor pool (main season). Adventure play area. Tennis. Fishing. Bicycle hire. Entertainment programme. Special environmental 'Acorn' activities for the family. WiFi (charged). Torches useful. No single sex groups. Off site: The Norfolk coast, Felbrigg Hall, the Walsingham Shrine and the Norfolk Broads National Park are nearby. Many bird and nature reserves.

Open: 10 February - 2 January.

Directions: On A148 road from Holt to Cromer, after High Kelling, turn left just before Bodham village (international sign) signed Weybourne. Follow road for about 1 mile to park. GPS: 52.92880, 1.14953

Charges guide

Per unit incl. electricity	£ 18,00 - £ 32,30
with full services	£ 23,45 - £ 39,00
dog (max. 2)	£ 3,10 - £ 5,15
awning	£ 2,10 - £ 5,15

Stanford Hall Caravan Park

Stanford Road, Swinford, Lutterworth LE17 6DH (Leicestershire)
t: **01788 860387** e: **stanfordpark@yahoo.co.uk**
alanrogers.com/UK3890 www.stanfordhall.co.uk/caravan.html

Accommodation: ☑Pitch ☐ Mobile home/chalet   ☐ Hotel/B&B   ☐ Apartment

This picturesque and tranquil site is ideally situated for an overnight stop where you are guaranteed a warm welcome and a pleasant stay. Formerly a Caravan Club site, it is set in the rural grounds of the Stanford Hall Estate, just a mile from the M1. There are 123 pitches (30 of which are seasonal), 80 on grass and 43 on hardstanding, all with 16A electricity. There are no shower or toilet facilities on the park, so your unit must be self contained. The site experiences high levels of repeat bookings so you are advised to contact them in advance of busy weekends to avoid being disappointed. Dogs are welcome but must be kept on a lead on the main site. A designated dog walk has been established through part of the estate woodland. Visitors staying on site (for two nights or more) receive free admission to the grounds of Stanford Hall during normal opening times, except on certain event days. There is a small charge for admission to the house.

Special offers
Book 2 nights or more for free admission to Stanford Hall (event days excluded).

You might like to know
A tranquil and picturesque site in the grounds of the Stanford Hall estate, which dates back to the 15th century.

☐ Environmental accreditation
☐ Reduced energy/water consumption policy
☐ Recycling and reusing policy
☑ Information about walking and cycling
☑ Footpaths within 500 m. of the site
☐ Fishing within 1 km.
☐ Riding or pony trekking within 1 km.
☐ Direct river or lake access
☐ Within 10 km. of an area of outstanding natural beauty or national park
☑ Wildlife haven (on site/within 1 km)
☐ Public transport
☑ Dogs welcome

Facilities: There are no toilets or shower facilities on site which means each unit must be totally self-contained. Tents are not accepted. A small shop sells basics. Newspapers can be ordered daily. Motorcaravan services. Picnic tables. Information room. Off site: Supermarkets and banks in Lutterworth. Warwick Castle 25 miles. NEC, Birmingham 30 miles. Stratford Upon Avon 35 miles. Silverstone, Rockingham and Mallory Race Circuits and Althorpe are within easy reach. Good location for walking and fishing. Jurassic Walk and the Grand Union Canal nearby.

Open: All year.

Directions: From the north on the M1 and from the M6 leave at exit 19 and at roundabout take first exit, signed Swinford, and follow signs for Stanford Hall. Site is on the left on Stanford Road. From east on A14, at the junction with the M1 roundabout, take exit to Swinford. From the south on the M1, leave at exit 18 onto the A428, A5 north and then follow signs for Stanford Hall. GPS: 52.406493, -1.149361

Charges guide

Per unit incl. 2 adults, 2 children and electricity	£ 14,00
extra person	£ 1,50
dog	free

Brynawelon Touring Park

Sarnau, Llandysul SA44 6RE (Ceredigion)
t: **01239 654584** e: **info@brynawelon.co.uk**
alanrogers.com/UK6005 **www.brynawelncp.co.uk**

Accommodation: ☑ Pitch ☐ Mobile home/chalet ☐ Hotel/B&B ☐ Apartment

Paul and Liz Cowton have turned Brynawelon into a friendly, attractive and well appointed campsite. It is in a stunning rural location within two miles of the Ceredigion coast with its beaches, and close to the River Teifi with plenty of water based activities. All the 40 pitches have electricity hook-ups and of these, 25 are serviced hardstanding pitches (electricity, water and waste). A number of all-weather pitches for tents have been added recently. The remainder are on level grass. The park has ample room for children to play, an enclosed play area, an indoor games room with TV, and a sauna next to reception. Buzzards, red kites, owls and the occasional eagle can be seen from the park. There is also a wide variety of small birds. A wide choice of beaches can be found along the coast, there are dolphin trips from New Quay ten miles away and white water rafting on the Teifi at Llandysul. The Teifi is also a well known canoeing and fishing river.

You might like to know

Combining the delights of the countryside and the West Wales coast, this is a tranquil, unspoilt area. The local sandy beach and pretty village are ideal for a relaxing stroll.

☐ Environmental accreditation
☐ Reduced energy/water consumption policy
☐ Recycling and reusing policy
☑ Information about walking and cycling
☑ Footpaths within 500 m. of the site
☐ Fishing within 1 km.
☐ Riding or pony trekking within 1 km.
☐ Direct river or lake access
☐ Within 10 km. of an area of outstanding natural beauty or national park
☑ Wildlife haven (on site/within 1 km)
☐ Public transport
☑ Dogs welcome

Facilities: Modern toilet block with toilets, showers, washbasins in cabins, two full suites in each side and a separate room for families and disabled visitors. Laundry/kitchen with washing machine, tumble dryer, ironing board and iron, fridge/freezer, microwave, kettle and toaster. Enclosed play area. Games room with table football, electronic games, TV and library. Sauna (charged). Dog walking area. WiFi (charged). Off site: Shops and pub 1 mile. Links with local farm shop (pre-order delivery, voucher scheme). Beach 1 mile. Fishing 2 miles. Golf and riding 3 miles. Dolphin trips at New Quay 10 miles. White-water rafting and canoeing at Llandysul 10 miles.

Open: March - 31 October.

Directions: Travelling north on the A487 from Cardigan turn right (southeast) at the crossroads in Sarnau village, signed Rhydlewis. Site is on the left after 650 yds. Note: the cross-country approach is not advised.
GPS: 52.13001, -4.45401

Charges guide

Per unit incl. 2 persons and electricity	£ 25,00
incl. 4 persons, hardstanding and services	£ 37,50

No credit cards.

Fforest Fields Touring Park

Hundred House, Builth Wells LD1 5RT (Powys)
t: 01982 570406 e: office@fforestfields.co.uk
alanrogers.com/UK6320 www.fforestfields.co.uk

Accommodation: ☑Pitch ☐ Mobile home/chalet ☐ Hotel/B&B ☐ Apartment

This secluded park is set on a family hill farm within seven acres in the heart of Radnorshire. This is simple country camping and caravanning at its best, with no clubhouse, swimming pool or games room. The facilities include 80 large pitches on level grass on a spacious and peaceful, carefully landscaped field by a stream. Electrical connections (mostly 16A) are available and there are 17 hardstanding pitches, also with electricity. Several additional areas without electricity are provided for tents. There are two new lakes, one for boating and fly fishing, the other for coarse fishing. George and Katie, the enthusiastic owners, have opened up much of the farm for woodland and moorland trails, which can be enjoyed with much wildlife to see. Indeed, wildlife is actively encouraged with nesting boxes for owls, songbirds and bats, by leaving field margins wild to encourage small mammals, and by yearly tree planting.

You might like to know

Why not try paragliding and experience the beauty of nature from the air?

☐ Environmental accreditation
☐ Reduced energy/water consumption policy
☑ Recycling and reusing policy
☑ Information about walking and cycling
☑ Footpaths within 500 m. of the site
☑ Fishing within 1 km.
☐ Riding or pony trekking within 1 km.
☐ Direct river or lake access
☐ Within 10 km. of an area of outstanding natural beauty or national park
☑ Wildlife haven (on site/within 1 km)
☐ Public transport
☑ Dogs welcome

Facilities: The toilet facilities are acceptable with baby bath, dishwashing and laundry facilities including washing machines and a dryer. Milk, eggs, orange juice and gas are sold in reception, otherwise there are few other on-site facilities. Fishing. Torches are useful. WiFi throughout. Off site: Pub at Hundred House village 1 mile. Bicycle hire and golf 5 miles. Riding 10 miles.

Open: Easter - October.

Directions: Park is 4 miles east of Builth Wells near the village of Hundred House on A481. Follow brown signs. Do not use postcode on sat nav. GPS: 52.17121, -3.31621

Charges guide

Per unit incl. 2 persons

and electricity	£ 16,00
extra person	£ 4,00
child (2-16 yrs)	£ 2,50
dog (max. 2)	free

No credit cards.

Pen-y-Bont Touring Park

Llangynog Road, Bala LL23 7PH (Gwynedd)
t: 01678 520549 e: penybont-bala@btconnect.co.uk
alanrogers.com/UK6340 www.penybont-bala.co.uk

Accommodation: ☑Pitch ☐ Mobile home/chalet ☐ Hotel/B&B ☐ Apartment

This is a pretty little park with 59 touring pitches, 47 of which have hardstanding. Connected by circular gravel roads, they are intermingled with trees and tall trees edge the site. Electricity connections (16A) are available, including 11 for tents, and there are 28 serviced pitches with hardstanding, electricity, water and drainage. There are also pitches for 25 seasonal units. The park entrance and the stone building that houses reception and the well stocked shop provide quite a smart image. With views of the Berwyn mountains, Pen-y-bont has a peaceful, attractive and useful location being the closest park to Bala town. Bala Lake is 100 yards and the park is three miles from the Welsh National White Water Centre, with Snowdonia on hand.

You might like to know

Bala Lake, close to the campsite, is the largest natural lake in Wales and offers all kinds of watersports and plenty of secluded spots to unwind.

- ☐ Environmental accreditation
- ☑ Reduced energy/water consumption policy
- ☑ Recycling and reusing policy
- ☑ Information about walking and cycling
- ☐ Footpaths within 500 m. of the site
- ☑ Fishing within 1 km.
- ☐ Riding or pony trekking within 1 km.
- ☐ Direct river or lake access
- ☐ Within 10 km. of an area of outstanding natural beauty or national park
- ☑ Wildlife haven (on site/within 1 km)
- ☐ Public transport
- ☑ Dogs welcome

Facilities: The toilet block includes washbasins in cubicles and spacious hot showers. Two new cubicles with washbasin and WC. Separate laundry room and an en-suite unit for disabled visitors, that doubles as a baby room, operated by key (£5 deposit). Outside covered area with fencing and concrete floor for dishwashing sinks and bins. Motorcaravan service point. Shop. Bicycle hire. Caravan storage. WiFi (charged). Off site: Fishing 200 yds. Boat launching, golf and riding 2 miles. Mon. market in Bala.

Open: 1 March - 31 October.

Directions: Park is 0.5 miles southeast of Bala village on the B4391. Bala is between Dolgellau and Conwen on the A494.
GPS: 52.901717, -3.590117

Charges guide

Per unit incl. 2 persons and electricity	£ 18,50 - £ 22,50
tent pitch incl. 2 persons	£ 15,00 - £ 20,00
extra person	£ 7,50
child (4-16 yrs)	£ 4,00
dog	£ 1,00

UNITED KINGDOM – Castle Douglas

Loch Ken Holiday Park

Parton, Castle Douglas DG7 3NE (Dumfries and Galloway)
t: 01644 470282 e: office@lochkenholidaypark.co.uk
alanrogers.com/UK6940 www.lochkenholidaypark.co.uk

Accommodation: ☑Pitch ☑Mobile home/chalet ☐ Hotel/B&B ☐ Apartment

Loch Ken Holiday Park sits right on the shore of the loch, adjacent to the RSPB bird reserve and the Galloway Forest Park – it is a peaceful haven in an area of outstanding beauty. This is a family owned park with 40 touring pitches and 33 caravan holiday homes, ten of which are for rent. The touring pitches, all with 10A electricity, are quite separate and are arranged in a mostly open-plan way on a large, neatly mown grass area beside the water. Some of this area is gently undulating. Mature trees border the park and provide an area for walking dogs. Site lighting is minimal so torches are advised. The spacious reception and well stocked shop are centrally located with a separate, well presented tourist information area. There are facilities for launching small boats, but these must be registered with the local council (at reception). This park is probably mostly suited to couples and families with older children who enjoy outdoor pursuits.

You might like to know

There are more than five mountain bike routes from site, suitable for all ability levels from beginners to those seeking a real challenge.

☐ Environmental accreditation
☐ Reduced energy/water consumption policy
☐ Recycling and reusing policy
☑ Information about walking and cycling
☑ Footpaths within 500 m. of the site
☑ Fishing within 1 km.
☐ Riding or pony trekking within 1 km.
☑ Direct river or lake access
☐ Within 10 km. of an area of outstanding natural beauty or national park
☑ Wildlife haven (on site/within 1 km)
☐ Public transport
☑ Dogs welcome

Facilities: The toilet block has been completely refurbished to modern standards and was exceptionally clean when we visited. Separate facilities in a modern Portacabin unit are provided in the tent area. Facilities for disabled visitors, Gas supplies. Well stocked shop. Good play area. Bicycles, canoes and dinghies for hire. Boat launching (permit from reception). Fishing (permit). Off site: Buses stop at the entrance, but are limited. Skiing 0.5 miles. Golf and riding 7 miles. Bars and restaurants in Castle Douglas 9 miles. Kirkcudbright 15 miles.

Open: 1 March - 31 October.

Directions: From Castle Douglas take the A713 north for 7 miles. Site entrance is on left in Parton. GPS: 55.0104, -4.05568

Charges guide

Per unit incl. 2 persons, 2 children and electricity	£ 17,00 - £ 21,00
tent, no electricity	£ 12,00 - £ 17,00
extra person	£ 2,00
dog	£ 2,00

The River Tilt Park

Golf Course Road, Blair Atholl, Pitlochry PH18 5TB (Perth and Kinross)
t: 01796 481467 e: stuart@rivertilt.co.uk
alanrogers.com/UK7295 www.rivertiltpark.co.uk

Accommodation: ☑ Pitch ☑ Mobile home/chalet ☐ Hotel/B&B ☐ Apartment

This good quality, family owned park is set on the banks of the River Tilt, a short walk from the village of Blair Atholl, where the 16th-century Blair Castle stands proud. There are 54 privately owned caravan holiday homes. Two central areas have been set aside for touring caravans, motorcaravans and tents, with 31 pitches mostly with hardstanding. Divided by mature shrubs and hedges, all have 10A electricity connections, 18 have water and a drain. One of the areas is reserved for dog owners and their pets. The Steadings Spa provides an indoor pool, solarium, steam room, spa pool and multigym, plus Waves hair salon. Also open to the public, there are charges for these facilities. The park also has an award winning restaurant. Adjacent are a riverside walk and a golf course. There may be some noise from the railway line that runs alongside the park.

You might like to know

Visitors love the working watermill, and shouldn't miss the Atholl Country Life Museum, which houses a unique collection of local artefacts including Scotlands only stuffed Highland cow.

- ☐ Environmental accreditation
- ☐ Reduced energy/water consumption policy
- ☐ Recycling and reusing policy
- ☑ Information about walking and cycling
- ☑ Footpaths within 500 m. of the site
- ☑ Fishing within 1 km.
- ☑ Riding or pony trekking within 1 km.
- ☐ Direct river or lake access
- ☐ Within 10 km. of an area of outstanding natural beauty or national park
- ☑ Wildlife haven (on site/within 1 km)
- ☐ Public transport
- ☑ Dogs welcome

Facilities: The purpose built toilet block is centrally situated (with key entry) and provides en-suite toilet and washbasin cabins and individual large preset showers, one suitable for disabled visitors. Baby facilities. Well equipped laundry. Motorcaravan service point. Bar and restaurant. Leisure spa complex with indoor pool, etc. Hair salon. Tennis. WiFi throughout (free). Max. 2 dogs per pitch. Off site: Private fishing and golf adjacent. Bicycle hire 0.5 miles. Riding 1.5 miles. Pitlochry with its famous salmon leap 6 miles. Bus or train from Blair Atholl.

Open: Two weeks after Easter - 10 November.

Directions: From the A9 just north of Pitlochry, take B8079 into Blair Atholl and follow signs for River Tilt. GPS: 56.76538, -3.83962

Charges guide

Per unit incl. 2 persons and electricity	£ 16,00 - £ 20,00
extra person	£ 1,50
child	£ 1,00
dog	£ 2,00

UNITED KINGDOM – Fort William

Glen Nevis Caravan Park

Glen Nevis, Fort William PH33 6SX (Highland)
t: 01397 702191 e: camping@glen-nevis.co.uk
alanrogers.com/UK7830 www.glen-nevis.co.uk

Accommodation: ☑ Pitch ☐ Mobile home/chalet ☐ Hotel/B&B ☐ Apartment

Just outside Fort William, in a most attractive and quiet situation with views of Ben Nevis, this spacious park is used by those on active pursuits as well as sightseeing tourists. It comprises eight quite spacious fields, divided between caravans, motorcaravans and tents (steel pegs required). It is licensed for 250 touring caravans but with no specific tent limits. The large touring pitches, many with hardstanding, are marked with wooden fence dividers, 174 with electricity (13A) and 100 also have water and drainage. The park becomes full in the peak months but there are vacancies each day. If reception is closed (possible in low season) you site yourself. There are regular security patrols at night in busy periods. The park's own modern restaurant and bar with good value bar meals is a short stroll from the park, open to all. A well managed park with bustling, but pleasing ambience, watched over by Ben Nevis. Around 1,000 acres of the Glen Nevis estate are open to see the wildlife and explore this lovely area.

You might like to know

The campsite is located at the foot of Ben Nevis, the highest mountain in the British isles. There are numerous ways to discover this scenic area including a gondola ride up Aonach Mor, a boat trip on Loch Linnhe or a day trip to Loch Ness.

☐ Environmental accreditation
☐ Reduced energy/water consumption policy
☑ Recycling and reusing policy
☑ Information about walking and cycling
☑ Footpaths within 500 m. of the site
☑ Fishing within 1 km.
☑ Riding or pony trekking within 1 km.
☐ Direct river or lake access
☐ Within 10 km. of an area of outstanding natural beauty or national park
☑ Wildlife haven (on site/within 1 km)
☐ Public transport
☐ Dogs welcome

Facilities: The four modern toilet blocks with showers (extra showers in two blocks); and units for visitors with disabilities. An excellent block in Nevis Park (one of the eight camping fields) has some washbasins in cubicles, showers, further facilities for disabled visitors, a second large laundry room and dishwashing sinks. Motorcaravan service point. Shop (Easter-mid Oct), barbecue area and snack bar (May-mid Sept). Play area on bark. Off site: Pony trekking, golf and fishing nearby.

Open: 15 March - 31 October.

Directions: Turn off A82 to east at roundabout just north of Fort William following camp sign. GPS: 56.804517, -5.073917

Charges guide

Per person	£1,80 - £ 3,00
child (5-15 yrs)	£ 1,00 - £ 1,60
pitch incl. awning	£ 8,30 - £ 11,40
serviced pitch plus	£ 11,80 - £ 15,40

Beara Camping The Peacock

Coornagillagh, Tuosist, Post Killarney (Co. Kerry)
t: 064 668 4287 e: bearacamping@eircom.net
alanrogers.com/IR9580 www.bearacamping.com

Accommodation: ☑Pitch ☑Mobile home/chalet ☑Hotel/B&B ☐ Apartment

Five minutes from Kenmare Bay, The Peacock is a unique location for campers who appreciate the natural world, where disturbance to nature is kept to a minimum. This five-acre site offers simple, clean and imaginative camping facilities. Located on the Ring of Beara, bordering the counties of Cork and Kerry, visitors will be treated with hospitality by a Dutch couple, Bert and Klaske van Bavel, almost more Irish than the Irish, who have made Ireland their home and run the site with their family. The variety of accommodation at Beara Camping includes a hostel, caravan holiday homes, secluded hardstanding pitches with electricity and level grass areas for tenting. In addition, there are cabins sleeping two or four people and hiker huts sleeping two, ideal to avoid a damp night or to dry out. Bert and Klaske love to share with visitors the unspoiled natural terrain, its wildlife, the sheltered community campfire and advice on the walking and hiking routes in the area.

You might like to know
Boat trips to see the seals start just 50 m. from the campsite.

☐ Environmental accreditation
☑ Reduced energy/water consumption policy
☑ Recycling and reusing policy
☑ Information about walking and cycling
☑ Footpaths within 500 m. of the site
☑ Fishing within 1 km.
☐ Riding or pony trekking within 1 km.
☐ Direct river or lake access
☑ Within 10 km. of an area of outstanding natural beauty or national park
☐ Wildlife haven (on site/within 1 km)
☑ Public transport
☑ Dogs welcome

Facilities: Three small blocks, plus facilities at the restaurant provide toilets, washbasins and free hot showers. Laundry service for a small fee. Campers' kitchens and sheltered eating area. Restaurant and takeaway (May-Oct). Pets are not permitted in rental accommodation or tents. Off site: Public transport from the gate during the summer months. Pub and shop 900 m. Riding 6 km. Golf 12 km. Boating, fishing and sea angling 200 m. Beach (pebble) 500 m.

Open: 1 April - 31 December.

Directions: From the N22, 17 km. east of Killarney, take the R569 south to Kenmare. In Kenmare take R571, Castletownbere road and site is 12 km. GPS: 51.8279, -9.7356

Charges guide

Per unit incl. 2 persons and electricity	€ 22,50
extra person	€ 3,50
child (0-10 yrs)	€ 2,00

The Apple Caravan Park

Moorstown, Cahir (Co. Tipperary)
t: 052 744 1459 e: con@theapplefarm.com
alanrogers.com/IR9410 www.theapplefarm.com

Accommodation: ☑ Pitch ☐ Mobile home/chalet ☐ Hotel/B&B ☐ Apartment

This fruit farm and campsite combination offers an idyllic country holiday venue in one of the most delightful situations imaginable. For tourers only, it is located off the N24, midway between Clonmel and Cahir. The park has 32 pitches in a secluded situation behind the barns and are mostly grass with 14 hardstandings and 25 electricity connections (13A, Europlug). Entrance is by way of a 300 m. drive flanked by the orchard fields and various non-fruit tree species, which are named and of interest to guests who are free to spend time walking the paths around the farm. When we visited, strawberries were being gathered – the best we had tasted all season – and award-winning apple juice, cordials, jams, etc. are also sold by Con and Noreen in the farm shop. Reception is housed with the other site facilities in a large farmyard barn. Although a rather unusual arrangement, it is central and effective. Cahir and Clonmel are of historic interest and the countryside boasts rivers, mountains and scenic drives.

You might like to know

Surrounded by abundant orchards, you can sit back and relax and try some of the produce from the farm shop, including, of course, apple juice and cider!

☐ Environmental accreditation
☐ Reduced energy/water consumption policy
☑ Recycling and reusing policy
☑ Information about walking and cycling
☑ Footpaths within 500 m. of the site
☐ Fishing within 1 km.
☐ Riding or pony trekking within 1 km.
☐ Direct river or lake access
☐ Within 10 km. of an area of outstanding natural beauty or national park
☑ Wildlife haven (on site/within 1 km)
☐ Public transport
☐ Dogs welcome

Facilities: Toilet facilities, kept very clean, quite modern in design and with heating, comprise showers, washbasins with mirrors, electric points, etc. in functional units occupying two corners of the large floor space. Facilities for disabled visitors. Also in the barn are dishwashing sinks, washing machine and a fridge/freezer for campers to use. Good drive-on motorcaravan service point. Good tennis court (free). Play area. Dogs only accepted by prior arrangement. Off site: Fishing, golf, bicycle hire and riding within 6 km.

Open: 1 May - 30 September.

Directions: Park is 300 m. off the main N24, 9.6 km. west of Clonmel, 6.4 km. east of Cahir. GPS: 52.37663, -7.84262

Charges guide

Per unit incl. 2 persons and electricity	€ 15,50
extra person	€ 6,50
child	€ 4,50

IRELAND – Caherdaniel

Wave Crest Touring Park

Caherdaniel (Co. Kerry)

t: 066 947 5188 e: wavecrest@eircom.net

alanrogers.com/IR9560 www.wavecrestcamping.com

Accommodation: ☑ Pitch ☐ Mobile home/chalet ☐ Hotel/B&B ☐ Apartment

It would be difficult to imagine a more dramatic location than Wave Crest's on the Ring of Kerry coast. Huge boulders and rocky outcrops tumble from the park entrance on the N70 down to the seashore which forms the most southern promontory on the Ring of Kerry. There are spectacular southward views from the park across Kenmare Bay to the Beara peninsula. Sheltering on grass patches in small coves that nestle between the rocks and shrubbery, are 65 hardstanding pitches and 20 on grass offering seclusion. Electricity connections are available (13A). This park would suit older people looking for a quiet, relaxed atmosphere. A unique feature is the TV room, an old stone farm building with a thatched roof. Its comfortable interior includes a stone fireplace heated by a converted cast iron marker buoy. Caherdaniel is known for its cheerful little pubs and distinguished restaurant. The Derrynane National Park Nature Reserve is only a few kilometres away, as is Derrynane Cove and Bay.

You might like to know

Boat launching and mooring are available for visitors who want to enjoy the Irish coast from the sea.

- ☑ Environmental accreditation
- ☑ Reduced energy/water consumption policy
- ☑ Recycling and reusing policy
- ☑ Information about walking and cycling
- ☐ Footpaths within 500 m. of the site
- ☐ Fishing within 1 km.
- ☑ Riding or pony trekking within 1 km.
- ☐ Direct river or lake access
- ☑ Within 10 km. of an area of outstanding natural beauty or national park
- ☑ Wildlife haven (on site/within 1 km)
- ☐ Public transport
- ☑ Dogs welcome

Facilities: Two blocks house the sanitary and laundry facilities and include hot showers on payment (€ 1). Small shop and takeaway service (June-Sept). Small play area. Fishing and boat launching. Off site: Riding 1 km. Bicycle hire and golf 10 km. Small beach near and Derrynane Hotel with bar and restaurant.

Open: All year.

Directions: On the N70 (Ring of Kerry), 1.5 km. east of Caherdaniel. GPS: 51.75881, -10.09112

Charges guide

Per unit incl. 2 persons and electricity	€ 27,00
extra person	€ 6,00
child	€ 2,00

Camping Le Roptai

Rue Roptai 34, B-5580 Ave et Auffe (Namur)
t: 084 388 319 e: info@leroptai.be
alanrogers.com/BE0850 www.leroptai.be

Accommodation: ☑Pitch ☑Mobile home/chalet ☐ Hotel/B&B ☐ Apartment

This family site was established in 1932 and can be found at the heart of the Ardennes, within easy reach of Dinant and Namur. This is a good site for an active holiday with a weekly programme on offer, including rock climbing, mountain biking, potholing and much more. There are 110 pitches and these are of a good size and mostly equipped with electricity. On-site amenities include a swimming pool, a well-stocked shop and a bar/snack bar. Le Roptai is open for a long season and is just closed during January. There are excellent footpaths around the site and the owners will be pleased to recommend routes. The pretty little village of Ave can be found around 1 km. from Le Roptai, and the larger village of Han-sur-Lesse is around 4 km. distant. There is an evening market at Han, as well as world-famous caves. The village is also home to the interesting Maison de la Vie Paysanne.

Special offers
Book a minimum of 1 week to receive a free hiking and cycling map of the Rochefort area.

You might like to know
Le Roptai is located in a beautiful woodland environment. The area is a haven for butterflies and has been visited by scientists from around the world. There is also a bird reserve in the village.

☑ Environmental accreditation
☐ Reduced energy/water consumption policy
☑ Recycling and reusing policy
☑ Information about walking and cycling
☑ Footpaths within 500 m. of the site
☐ Fishing within 1 km.
☐ Riding or pony trekking within 1 km.
☐ Direct river or lake access
☑ Within 10 km. of an area of outstanding natural beauty or national park
☑ Wildlife haven (on site/within 1 km)
☑ Public transport
☑ Dogs welcome

Facilities: Shop. Snack bar. Bar. Takeaway food. Swimming pool. Paddling pool. Play area. Tourist information. Activity programme. Mobile homes for rent. Off site: Cycle and walking tracks. Canoeing. Caves at Han-sur-Lesse.

Open: 1 February - 31 December.

Directions: From the E411 motorway (Brussels - Namur) take exit 23 (Wellin - Han-sur-Lesse) and follow signs to Han-sur-Lesse. Continue to Ave and turn left at the church, following signs to the site (1 km. further). GPS: 50.11128, 5.13376

Charges guide

Per unit incl. 2 persons and electricity	€ 18,80 - € 26,00
extra person	€ 2,80 - € 4,00
child (5-15 yrs)	€ 2,10 - € 3,00
dog	€ 1,70

Panoramacamping Petite Suisse

Al Bounire 27, B-6960 Dochamps (Luxembourg)
t: 084 444 030   e: info@petitesuisse.be
alanrogers.com/BE0735   www.petitesuisse.be

Accommodation: ☑Pitch ☑Mobile home/chalet ☐ Hotel/B&B ☐ Apartment

This quiet site is set in the picturesque countryside of the Belgium Ardennes, a region in which rivers flow through valleys bordered by vast forests where horses are still usefully employed. Set on a southerly slope, the site is mostly open and offers wide views of the surrounding countryside. The 193 touring pitches, all with 10A electricity, are either on open sloping ground or in terraced rows with hedges between the rows, and with trees providing some separation. Gravel roads provide access around the site. To the right of the entrance barrier a large wooden building houses reception, a bar and a restaurant. Close by is an attractive, heated outdoor swimming pool with wide terraces surrounded by grass. Behind this is a large play area adjoining a small terrace. Although the site has many activities on offer, the opportunity should not be missed to make excursions into the countryside. The villages are filled with houses built from the local stone and small inviting bars and restaurants. Member of the Ardenne and Gaume Group.

You might like to know

The Ardennes Rangers programme teaches children about nature and the local area. There are many wildlife parks, caves and mines to visit in the region.

☐ Environmental accreditation
☐ Reduced energy/water consumption policy
☐ Recycling and reusing policy
☑ Information about walking and cycling
☑ Footpaths within 500 m. of the site
☑ Fishing within 1 km.
☐ Riding or pony trekking within 1 km.
☐ Direct river or lake access
☐ Within 10 km. of an area of outstanding natural beauty or national park
☐ Wildlife haven (on site/within 1 km)
☐ Public transport
☑ Dogs welcome

Facilities: All the facilities that one would expect of a large site are available. Showers are free, washbasins both open and in cabins. Baby room. Laundry room with washing machines and dryers. Shop. Restaurant, bar and takeaway. Heated outdoor swimming pool (1/5-1/9), paddling pool and slide. Sports field. Tennis. Bicycle hire. Playground and club for children. Entertainment programme (24/4-1/11 plus 24/12-3/1). Varied activity programme, including archery, canoeing, climbing, abseiling and walking. WiFi (free). Max. 1 dog. Off site: La Roche en Ardennes and Baraque de Fraiture (ski resort) 10 km. Golf 20 km.

Open: All year.

Directions: From the E25/A26 autoroute (Liège - Luxembourg) take exit 50 then the N89 southwest towards La Roche. After 8 km. turn right (north) on N841 to Dochamps where site is signed. GPS: 50.23127, 5.62583

Charges guide

Per unit incl. 2 persons and electricity	€ 23,00 - € 30,50
extra person (over 4 yrs)	€ 4,50 - € 5,00
dog (max. 1)	€ 4,25 - € 5,00

Camping Auf Kengert

L-7633 Larochette-Medernach
t: 837186 e: info@kengert.lu
alanrogers.com/LU7640 www.kengert.lu

Accommodation: ☑ Pitch ☑ Mobile home/chalet ☐ Hotel/B&B ☐ Apartment

A friendly welcome awaits you at this peacefully situated, family run site, 2 km. from Larochette, which is 24 km. northeast of Luxembourg city, providing 180 individual pitches, all with electricity. Some in a very shaded woodland setting, on a slight slope with fairly narrow access roads. There are also eight hardened pitches for motorcaravans on a flat area of grass, complete with motorcaravan service facilities. Further tent pitches are in an adjacent and more open meadow area. There are also site owned wooden chalets for rent. This site is popular in season, so early arrival is advisable, or you can reserve. The pleasant swimming pool is overlooked by a terrace with a well-stocked shop, a restaurant and bar behind and a delightful children's indoor play area. In the meadow at the side of the site is a large sand-based adventure play park plus table tennis and table football. Beyond that is a 'barefoot woodland walk' along which you can tread on a variety of natural surfaces - reflexology on the go!

Special offers
Please see website for details of special offers.

You might like to know
A barefoot walking track starts direct from the campsite, and nearby you can join the Mullerthal Trail hiking track to explore Luxembourg's Little Switzerland.

☑ Environmental accreditation
☑ Reduced energy/water consumption policy
☑ Recycling and reusing policy
☑ Information about walking and cycling
☑ Footpaths within 500 m. of the site
☐ Fishing within 1 km.
☐ Riding or pony trekking within 1 km.
☐ Direct river or lake access
☑ Within 10 km. of an area of outstanding natural beauty or national park
☐ Wildlife haven (on site/within 1 km)
☑ Public transport
☑ Dogs welcome

Facilities: The well maintained sanitary block in two parts includes a modern, heated unit with some washbasins in cubicles, and excellent, fully equipped cubicles for disabled visitors. The showers, facilities for babies, additional WCs and washbasins, plus laundry room are located below the central building which houses the shop, bar and restaurant. Motorcaravan services. Gas supplies. Indoor and outdoor play areas. Solar heated swimming pool (Easter-30/9). Paddling pool. WiFi. Off site: Bicycle hire. Golf, fishing and riding 8 km.

Open: 1 March - 8 November.

Directions: From Larochette take the CR118/N8 (towards Mersch) and just outside town turn right on CR119 towards Schrondweiler, site is 2 km. on right. GPS: 49.79992, 6.19817

Charges guide

Per unit incl. 2 persons and electricity	€ 20,00 - € 32,00
extra person	€ 9,00 - € 15,00
child (4-17 yrs)	€ 5,00 - € 7,00
dog	€ 1,25

Camping Kautenbach

An der Weierbach, L-9663 Kautenbach
t: 950 303 e: info@campingkautenbach.lu
alanrogers.com/LU7830 www.campingkautenbach.lu

Accommodation: ☑Pitch ☑Mobile home/chalet ☐ Hotel/B&B ☐ Apartment

Kautenbach is an all-year site in the heart of the Luxembourg Ardennes. The site was established over 50 years ago and although in an idyllic location, it is less than a mile from a railway station with regular trains to Luxembourg city to the south. There are 135 touring pitches here, mostly of a good size and with reasonable shade. Most pitches have electrical connections (10A). This is excellent walking country with many tracks around the site. The site managers will be happy to recommend walks for all abilities. Kautenbach has an attractive bistro style restaurant, specialising in local cuisine, as well as a large selection of whiskies! The site has direct river access and fishing is popular (small charge applicable). During the high season, a wide range of activities are organised along with a lively children's club.

You might like to know
Kautenbach is hidden away in a beautiful valley on the banks of the River Clerve, in an area renowned for walking.

- ☑ Environmental accreditation
- ☑ Reduced energy/water consumption policy
- ☑ Recycling and reusing policy
- ☑ Information about walking and cycling
- ☑ Footpaths within 500 m. of the site
- ☑ Fishing within 1 km.
- ☐ Riding or pony trekking within 1 km.
- ☑ Direct river or lake access
- ☑ Within 10 km. of an area of outstanding natural beauty or national park
- ☐ Wildlife haven (on site/within 1 km)
- ☑ Public transport
- ☑ Dogs welcome

Facilities: Two toilet blocks with open style controllable washbasins and showers, baby changing. Facilities for disabled visitors (key). Dishwashing and laundry. Shop for basics (high season, bread to order). Restaurant, bar/snack bar. Direct river access. Fishing. Children's playground. Tourist information. Mobile homes for rent. Internet café. Off site: Walking and cycle trails. Railway station 500 m. Caves at Consdorf. Cathedral at Echternach.

Open: All year.

Directions: Head south from Namur on the A4 and then join the N4 (junction 15). Continue on the N4 to Bastogne and then join the N84 towards Wiltz. Follow signs to Kautenbach on the CR331 and the site is well signposted from here. GPS: 49.95387, 6.0273

Charges guide

Per unit incl. 2 persons and electricity	€ 19,75 - € 23,75
extra person	€ 5,80
child (18 months-12 yrs)	€ 3,75
dog	€ 2,50

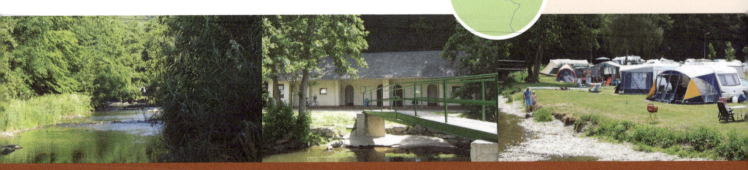

Camping Val d'Or

Um Gaertchen 2, L-9747 Enscherange
t: 920 691   e: valdor@pt.lu
alanrogers.com/LU7770   www.valdor.lu

Accommodation: ☑ Pitch   ☑ Mobile home/chalet   ☐ Hotel/B&B   ☐ Apartment

Camping Val d'Or is one of those small family-run countryside sites where you easily find yourself staying longer than planned. Set on lush meadowland under a scattering of trees, the site is divided into two by the tree-lined Clerve river as it winds its way slowly through the site. A footbridge goes some way to joining the site together and there are two entrances for vehicles. There are 76 unmarked, level grass touring pitches, all with electricity (4A) and with some tree shade. There are open views of the surrounding countryside with its wooded hills. The site's Dutch owners speak good English. Fred van Donk is active in the Luxembourg tourist industry. He is happy to give advice about this interesting, attractive and, to most people, less well known region of Europe which is within easy reach of the Channel ports and Holland. The friendly bar is a popular meeting point. The site participates in the 'Wanderhütten' scheme providing wooden huts for rent to hikers. A local railway passes the site but it is not obtrusive.

You might like to know

During the high season, there are guided walks to ensure that you make the most of the forest.

☑ Environmental accreditation
☑ Reduced energy/water consumption policy
☑ Recycling and reusing policy
☑ Information about walking and cycling
☑ Footpaths within 500 m. of the site
☐ Fishing within 1 km.
☐ Riding or pony trekking within 1 km.
☑ Direct river or lake access
☐ Within 10 km. of an area of outstanding natural beauty or national park
☑ Wildlife haven (on site/within 1 km)
☐ Public transport
☑ Dogs welcome

Facilities: Heated sanitary block where some facilities are found, others including some showers are located under cover, outside. Showers are token operated, washbasins open style. Facilities may be stretched in high season. Laundry room. Gas supplies. Bar (all day in high season). Takeaway (high season except Sundays). Swimming and paddling in river. Three play areas (one with waterways, waterwheel and small pool). Bicycle hire. WiFi (charged). Max. 1 dog. Off site: Fishing and golf 10 km.

Open: 1 April - 1 November.

Directions: From A26/E25 (Liège - Luxembourg) exit 54 travel to Bastogne. From Bastogne take N84/N15 towards Diekirch for 15 km. At crossroads turn left (northeast) towards Wiltz following signs for Clervaux. Pass though Wiltz and entering Weidingen there is a VW garage on the right; 500 m. after the garage turn right on the Wilderwiltz road. In Wilderwiltz follow signs for small village of Enscherange where site is signed. GPS: 50.00017, 5.99106

Charges guide

Per unit incl. 2 persons and electricity	€ 22,00
extra person	€ 5,00
child (0-15 yrs)	€ 2,00

No credit cards.

NETHERLANDS – Weidum

Camping WeidumerHout

Dekemawei 9, NL-9024 BE Weidum (Friesland)
t: 0582 519 888 e: welkom@weidumerhout.nl
alanrogers.com/NL5715 www.weidumerhout.nl

Accommodation: ☑Pitch ☑Mobile home/chalet ☑Hotel/B&B ☐ Apartment

Camping WeidumerHout is a member of the Kleine Groene Campings group, literally 'small green campsites'. It has a beautiful rural location, close to the historic village of Weidum. There are 48 well spaced pitches (150 sq.m) with 10A electricity and two with hardstanding. The owner makes sure that all visitors can enjoy the great views over either the countryside or the river that runs past the site. The site's fully equipped sauna (on payment) will add to your relaxation – owner Eddy de Boer will describe the benefits of a good sauna. The campsite is combined with a comfortable hotel and welcoming, stylish restaurant. Try one of the daily, high quality meals created with local produce, maybe washed down with a glass of Us Heit Friesian beer. The site has its own water purifying system and tries to operate in an environmentally friendly way. The river Zwette running past the site is part of the famous 11 city skating tour and you are more than welcome to bring a boat.

Special offers

Amenities available to guests on the site include the Tevens Hotel restaurant and sauna.

You might like to know

The site is located on the historic Eleven Cities Tour route for ice skaters, near Leeuwarden, Sneek and Franeker. The skating race has not taken place since 1997 due to poor weather conditions, but the route can also be followed by bicycle.

☑ Environmental accreditation
☑ Reduced energy/water consumption policy
☑ Recycling and reusing policy
☑ Information about walking and cycling
☑ Footpaths within 500 m. of the site
☑ Fishing within 1 km.
☐ Riding or pony trekking within 1 km.
☑ Direct river or lake access
☐ Within 10 km. of an area of outstanding natural beauty or national park
☐ Wildlife haven (on site/within 1 km)
☑ Public transport
☑ Dogs welcome

Facilities: Heated sanitary block with toilets, showers and basins. Baby room. Washing machine and dryer. Bar and restaurant. Sauna. Solarium. Library. Bicycle hire. Beach access plus fishing and boat launching. Canoe hire. WiFi (free). Fitness equipment. Torch useful. Off site: Shop and bus stop 800 m. Riding 5 km. Sailing 8km. Golf 12 km.

Open: All year, excl. Christmas - 1 January.

Directions: From Leeuwarden head south on the A32 and follow signs for Weidum. Just before entering the village, the site is on the right. GPS: 53.14906, 5.76166

Charges guide

Per unit incl. 2 persons and electricity	€ 21,25
extra person (over 2 yrs)	€ 5,75
dog	€ 2,00

Camping Waalstrand

Waaldijk 23A, NL-6691 MB Gendt (Gelderland)
t: 0481 421 604 e: info@waalstrand.nl
alanrogers.com/NL5823 www.waalstrand.nl

Accommodation: ☑Pitch ☑Mobile home/chalet ☐ Hotel/B&B ☐ Apartment

Camping Waalstrand lies just outside the village of Gendt. It is stretched out along the banks of the River Waal and many of the pitches have good views of the wide range of boats plying the river. Surrounding the campsite is an excellent nature reserve, an extensive delta with many walks and cycle routes. This is a quiet campsite with no organised entertainment. There are 150 average size, level, unshaded, grassy/sandy pitches with 90 for touring. All pitches have 6A electricity and a TV hookup. Access is good for large outfits. The German border is close by and within 16 km. are the well known ancient cities of Arnhem and Nijmegen with their interesting old quarters and historical connections to World War Two. The nature reserve surrounding the campsite is called the Gelderse Poort, a collective name for the ribbon of river dunes, lowland forests and meadows alongside the river banks.

You might like to know

Set in the national park of Gelderse Poort, this site offers pitches right on the river with unique views of river dunes, Galloway cattle and Konik horses. There are hikes and cycling trips from the campsite, with bicycle hire available.

- ☐ Environmental accreditation
- ☑ Reduced energy/water consumption policy
- ☑ Recycling and reusing policy
- ☑ Information about walking and cycling
- ☑ Footpaths within 500 m. of the site
- ☑ Fishing within 1 km.
- ☐ Riding or pony trekking within 1 km.
- ☑ Direct river or lake access
- ☑ Within 10 km. of an area of outstanding natural beauty or national park
- ☑ Wildlife haven (on site/within 1 km)
- ☑ Public transport
- ☑ Dogs welcome

Facilities: Modern clean toilet block with all necessary facilities. Washing machine/dryer. Café. Outdoor swimming pool. Children's play area. Boules. Table tennis. Large chess set. Sandy river beach, small boat ramp. Bike hire. Motorhome services. Fishing. WiFi (charged). Dogs are welcome but just on a small part of the site and only one dog per pitch. Visitors may not bring dogs. Off site: German border. Gelderse Poort nature reserve. Arnhem, many ancient buildings, shops, bars, cafes, zoo. World War II museum. Nijmegen, Holland's oldest city. Many marked walks and cycle tracks. Boating on river. River ferries.

Open: 1 April - 2 October.

Directions: Leave A15 motorway at Bemmel between Nijmegen and Arnhem, signed Gendt. Follow ANWB signs for Waalstrand – do not drive through the narrow streets in Gendt (7 km. from motorway). GPS: 51.87597, 5.98897

Charges guide

Per unit incl. 2 persons and electricity	€ 25,00
dog	€ 3,00

Camping De Roos

Beerzerweg 10, NL-7736 PJ Beerze-Ommen (Overijssel)
t: 0523 251 234 e: info@campingderoos.nl
alanrogers.com/NL5980 www.campingderoos.nl

Accommodation: ☑Pitch ☑Mobile home/chalet ☐ Hotel/B&B ☐ Apartment

De Roos is a family run site in an area of outstanding natural beauty, truly a nature lover's campsite, immersed in an atmosphere of tranquillity. It is situated in Overijssel's Vecht Valley, a unique region set in a river dune landscape on the River Vecht. The river and its tributary wind their way unhurriedly around and through this spacious campsite. It is a natural setting that the owners have carefully preserved. The 285 pitches and necessary amenities have been blended into the landscape with great care. Pitches, many with electricity hook-up (6A), are naturally sited, some behind blackthorn thickets, in the shadow of an old oak, or in a clearing scattered with wild flowers. For some there are lovely views over the Vecht river. De Roos is a car-free campsite during peak periods – vehicles must be parked at the car park, except on arrival and departure. The enthusiastic owners have compiled walking and cycling routes which are written in English and follow the ever-changing countryside of the Vecht Valley.

Special offers
Spring package: 6 April - 1 July for € 550.
June package: 1 June - 1 July for € 280.

You might like to know
This car-free site has a tea shop and a grocery store. You can swim in the river, and bicycle hire is available.

☑ Environmental accreditation
☑ Reduced energy/water consumption policy
☑ Recycling and reusing policy
☑ Information about walking and cycling
☑ Footpaths within 500 m. of the site
☑ Fishing within 1 km.
☐ Riding or pony trekking within 1 km.
☑ Direct river or lake access
☑ Within 10 km. of an area of outstanding natural beauty or national park
☑ Wildlife haven (on site/within 1 km)
☐ Public transport
☐ Dogs welcome

Facilities: Four well maintained sanitary blocks are kept fresh and clean. The two larger blocks are heated and include baby bath/shower and wash cabins. Launderette. Motorcaravan services. Gas supplies. Health food shop and tea room (1/5-1/9). Bicycle hire. Boules. Several small playgrounds and field for kite flying. River swimming. Fishing. Dogs are not accepted (and cats must be kept on a lead!). Torch useful. Off site: Riding 6 km. Golf 10 km.

Open: 8 April - 2 October.

Directions: Leave A28 at Ommen exit 21 and join N340 for 19 km. to Ommen. Turn right at traffic lights over bridge and immediately left on local road towards Beerze. Site on left after 7 km. just after Beerze village sign. GPS: 52.51078, 6.51537

Charges guide

Per unit incl. 2 persons and electricity	€ 17,30 - € 20,30
extra person	€ 2,90 - € 3,60
child (under 3 yrs)	free

Campingpark De Barkhoorn

Beetserweg 6, NL-9551 VE Sellingen (Groningen)
t: 0599 322510 e: info@barkhoorn.nl
alanrogers.com/NL6115 www.barkhoorn.nl

Accommodation: ☑ Pitch ☑ Mobile home/chalet ☐ Hotel/B&B ☐ Apartment

Camping De Barkhoorn is located in the Westerwolde southeast of Groningen. The campsite is surrounded by vast forests and heathland, interspersed with beautiful ponds. A car-free site, there are 152 touring pitches (including 13 'comfort' pitches and pitches for motorcaravans, 82 permanent pitches and six cabins for rent. Tall trees provide plenty of shade. This is a pleasant family campsite, ideal for families with children. There are spacious green areas, and in the holidays a recreation team provides entertainment and activities. There is a large natural recreational lake where you can swim. Adjacent to the site are a heated outdoor pool, an outdoor theatre and tennis courts. Many hiking and bicycle trails lead from the site and there are opportunities for fishing, mountain biking and canoeing. The Westerwolde area is rich in nature, culture and history. The German border is nearby.

You might like to know

Campingpark De Barkhoorn lies in Westerwolde, a landscape with a rich historical and cultural heritage, which can be explored both on foot and by canoe. Choose from around 30 different walks.

☐ Environmental accreditation
☑ Reduced energy/water consumption policy
☐ Recycling and reusing policy
☑ Information about walking and cycling
☑ Footpaths within 500 m. of the site
☑ Fishing within 1 km.
☐ Riding or pony trekking within 1 km.
☑ Direct river or lake access
☑ Within 10 km. of an area of outstanding natural beauty or national park
☐ Wildlife haven (on site/within 1 km)
☑ Public transport
☑ Dogs welcome

Facilities: Four sanitary buildings including one without hot water. Private facilities to rent. Facilities for disabled visitors. Launderette. Shop. Bar and terrace. Restaurant. Snack bar. Swimming pool with slide and toddlers' pool. Play areas. Recreation lake with beach. Sports field. Minigolf. Tennis. Bowling and other activities. Bicycle hire. Fishing. Canoeing. WiFi. Cabins to rent.

Open: 1 April - 31 October.

Directions: Follow signs from Zwolle, Hoogeveen and Emmen for Ter Apel. Sellingen is on the main road between Ter Apel and Winschoten, 2 km. from the centre of Sellingen. Follow site signs from the village.
GPS: 52.946406, 7.131192

Charges guide

Per unit incl. 2 persons and electricity	€ 17,50 - € 22,50
dog	€ 3,00

NETHERLANDS – Gasselte

Camping de Berken

Borgerweg 23, NL-9462 RA Gasselte (Drenthe)
t: 0599 564 255 e: info@campingdeberken.nl
alanrogers.com/NL6128 www.campingdeberken.nl

Accommodation: ☑Pitch ☑Mobile home/chalet ☐ Hotel/B&B ☐ Apartment

De Berken is an established site with well laid out pitches on grass fields with some trees. The site has 161 pitches of which 95 are for touring units. All have electricity, water and a drain, and there are 18 with private sanitary facilities. On site you will find a small shop for basic supplies, a recreation hall with an indoor playground and boules. A restaurant is 200 m. from the entrance. A countryside site, there are many possibilities for walking and cycling through nature reserves. In high season, an entertainment team keeps everyone busy. Close to the site is the Drouwenerzand moorland nature reserve and less than 2 km. away is the Nije Hemelriek with clear, open water for swimming. There are indoor and outdoor pools in Borger. However, the main attractions here are the tranquil atmosphere and a friendly welcome.

Special offers

High season offer: 7 nights for € 110
(for a comfort pitch including 16A electricity, water, drainage and TV connection).
Low season offer: 7 nights for € 105.

You might like to know

For your comfort and convenience there are a number of pitches with private bathroom. Hikers and cyclists will appreciate the routes starting directly from the site.

☐ Environmental accreditation
☑ Reduced energy/water consumption policy
☑ Recycling and reusing policy
☑ Information about walking and cycling
☑ Footpaths within 500 m. of the site
☐ Fishing within 1 km.
☑ Riding or pony trekking within 1 km.
☐ Direct river or lake access
☐ Within 10 km. of an area of outstanding natural beauty or national park
☑ Wildlife haven (on site/within 1 km)
☑ Public transport
☑ Dogs welcome

Facilities: Two heated modern toilet blocks with toilets, preset hot showers, family shower rooms and baby room. Shop for basics. Indoor playground. Full entertainment programme in high season. Internet access. Off site: Bar and restaurant 200 m. Nije Hemelriek for swimming 2 km. Pool complex 5 km.

Open: 1 April - 23 October.

Directions: From the N33 Groningen - Emmen take exit for Borger. Continue to Drouwen and site is on the right just after Drouwen and well signed. GPS: 52.96476, 6.78934

Charges guide

Per unit incl. 2 persons and electricity (plus meter)	€ 19,00 - € 21,00
with own sanitary unit	€ 25,00 - € 27,50
extra person	€ 3,50
dog	€ 3,00

Camping Meistershof

Lheebroek 33, NL-7991 PM Dwingeloo (Drenthe)
t: 0521 597 278 e: info@meistershof.nl
alanrogers.com/NL6147 www.meistershof.nl

Accommodation: ☑Pitch ☐ Mobile home/chalet ☐ Hotel/B&B ☐ Apartment

Meistershof is a small, interesting site with only 157 pitches, all for tourers. Developed on a former farm, the buildings have retained their original style, which gives the site a rustic look and feel. This, and the fact that the site is partly car free, ensures a relaxing holiday in beautiful, natural surroundings. The numbered pitches are level and arranged on grassy fields with paved access lanes. They are separated by a variety of hedges and have shade from mature trees, and 10A electricity. There are 40 pitches with electricity, water and drainage; some have hardstandings or private sanitary facilities. The terrain looks very well cared for and is close to the Dwingelderveld National Park where there are plenty of opportunities for walking and cycling. The owners of this well kept site are keen to preserve nature and all electricity comes from 'green' sources. They organise excursions with a guide through the nature reserve. A covered playground is to the front of the site and some fields have covered picnic areas.

You might like to know

In the immediate vicinity, you will find several places of interest such as the megalithic monuments, the planetarium and cinedome, and the National Park Information Centre.

☐ Environmental accreditation
☐ Reduced energy/water consumption policy
☑ Recycling and reusing policy
☑ Information about walking and cycling
☑ Footpaths within 500 m. of the site
☐ Fishing within 1 km.
☐ Riding or pony trekking within 1 km.
☐ Direct river or lake access
☑ Within 10 km. of an area of outstanding natural beauty or national park
☑ Wildlife haven (on site/within 1 km)
☐ Public transport
☑ Dogs welcome

Facilities: New, stylish toilet block at the centre of the site with superb facilities. Toilets, washbasins (open style and in cabins) and controllable hot showers (charged). Toilets and basins for children. Facilities for disabled visitors. Family shower room. Baby room. Laundry. Shop for basics. Snack bar. Playing field. Playground and covered play area. Minigolf. Boules. Excursions into Dwingelderveld. WiFi (charged).

Open: 1 April - 30 September.

Directions: From the A28 take exit 29 (Dwingeloo) and continue towards town. Site is signed before Dwingeloo and is in the village of Lheebroek. GPS: 52.845746, 6.427469

Charges guide

Per unit incl. 2 persons and electricity	€ 24,15
extra person	€ 4,10
child (1-10 yrs)	€ 3,50
dog	€ 3,00

Molecaten Park De Koerberg

Koerbergseweg 4/1, NL-8181 LL Heerde (Gelderland)
t: 0578 699 810 e: info@koerberg.nl
alanrogers.com/NL6355 www.molecaten.nl/dekoerberg

Accommodation: ☑Pitch ☑Mobile home/chalet ☐ Hotel/B&B ☐ Apartment

De Koerberg is a member of the Molecaten group and is located in the extensive Veluwe national park. This is a spacious site with large, well shaded pitches. Special hiker's pitches and simple cabins are available. Rentable accommodation includes safari style tents, and luxury mobile homes. The Dovecote restaurant has recently been added to the list of site amenities and offers a tempting range of local dishes (including takeaway meals). Breakfast can be delivered to your pitch if you wish. A bowling centre is also available and is great fun for a night out with a difference. A lively programme of activities and entertainment is arranged in high season. A children's club is held with many activities organised by the site's mascots, Molly and Caatje. Off site, there's plenty to do including a chocolate workshop and a bakery museum. The Kröller-Müller Van Gogh museum at Otterlo houses the world's second largest collection of the artist's work and is highly recommended.

You might like to know

The adjacent forest and wild moorland dotted with sheep make this area especially popular with nature lovers.

- ☐ Environmental accreditation
- ☐ Reduced energy/water consumption policy
- ☑ Recycling and reusing policy
- ☑ Information about walking and cycling
- ☑ Footpaths within 500 m. of the site
- ☐ Fishing within 1 km.
- ☐ Riding or pony trekking within 1 km.
- ☐ Direct river or lake access
- ☑ Within 10 km. of an area of outstanding natural beauty or national park
- ☑ Wildlife haven (on site/within 1 km)
- ☑ Public transport
- ☑ Dogs welcome

Facilities: Swimming pool. Shop. Bar, restaurant and takeaway food. Play area. Tennis. Football. Bowling alley. Entertainment and activity programme. Mobile homes and chalets to rent. Off site: Riding. Cycle and walking tracks. Kröller-Müller museum.

Open: 1 April - 30 October.

Directions: Heading south from Zwolle, leave A50 motorway at exit 28 and follow signs to Heerde. Then follow signs to the site. GPS: 52.40965, 6.051149

Charges guide

Per unit incl. 2 persons and electricity	€ 19,00 - € 25,00
dog (max. 1)	€ 3,90

Molecaten Park Landgoed

Koeweg 1, NL-8051 PM Hattem (Gelderland)
t: 0384 447 044 e: info@landgoedmolecaten.nl
alanrogers.com/NL6357 www.molecaten.nl/landgoedmolecaten

Accommodation: ☑Pitch ☑Mobile home/chalet ☐ Hotel/B&B ☐ Apartment

Landgoed Molecaten can be found amongst old beech and oak trees on the southern side of the fortified town of Hattem. This is a tranquil site with large pitches, surrounded by a variety of mature trees which provide plenty of privacy and shade. There are 130 hectares of woodland, flora and fauna here. Children can safely explore the woods – ideal for 'hide and seek'. A pair of owls have been resident here for many years and are often seen at twilight. Rentable accommodation includes a Boshuus, a specially designed chalet for four people, perfect for walkers and cyclists. An indoor and outdoor swimming pool can be found within easy walking distance. A number of theme parks are also close at hand, notably Walibi World, Julianatoren and Ecodrome. The Harderwijk dolphinarium is also excellent. There are more than 1,600 km. of cycle and walking tracks (some guided tours are available). For golfers there is a 9-hole golf centre and a pitch and putt course.

You might like to know

Surrounded by ancient beech and oak forest, the sound of birds singing is never far away.

☐ Environmental accreditation
☐ Reduced energy/water consumption policy
☑ Recycling and reusing policy
☑ Information about walking and cycling
☑ Footpaths within 500 m. of the site
☐ Fishing within 1 km.
☐ Riding or pony trekking within 1 km.
☐ Direct river or lake access
☑ Within 10 km. of an area of outstanding natural beauty or national park
☑ Wildlife haven (on site/within 1 km)
☐ Public transport
☑ Dogs welcome

Facilities: Snack bar with terrace. Play areas. Volleyball. Bicycle hire. GPS tours. Activity and entertainment programme. Off site: Cycling and walking tracks. Walibi World. Harderwijk and dolphinarium.

Open: 1 April - 3 October.

Directions: From the A50 motorway take exit 30 and follow signs towards Apeldoorn (Hattem/Hessenweg). Then follow directions to Hattem. Upon arrival here, continue ahead on to Hessenweg. Site is signed from here. GPS: 52.466955, 6.058115

Charges guide

Per unit incl. 2 persons and electricity	€ 14,50
extra person	€ 2,90
child (2-10 yrs)	€ 1,90
dog	€ 1,90

Camping De Grote Altena

Waaldijk 39, NL-6678 MC Oosterhout (Gelderland)
t: 0481 481 200 e: info@campingdegrotealtena.nl
alanrogers.com/NL6395 www.campingdegrotealtena.nl

Accommodation: ☑Pitch ☑Mobile home/chalet ☐ Hotel/B&B ☐ Apartment

This campsite is in a unique location on the river Waal and has 160 spacious pitches, half of which are situated right beside the river and have fabulous views. There are 25 permanent pitches and 60 seasonal pitches, leaving 75 for touring with 6A electricity. A separate field, with a fish pond, is available for short stays. The playground with open-air chess and trampoline is popular with children. De Grote Altena is ideal for nature lovers who enjoy peace and space. The attractive cities of Arnhem and Nijmegen are both within easy reach. The site lies at the heart of the Betuwe, a typically Dutch region with rolling meadows and river dikes. De Grote Altena is popular with anglers, with a small fishing pond as well as direct access to the Waal. There is a snack bar on site, with a terrace offering fine river views. Off site, the De Altena restaurant is highly rated. Fresh bread can be ordered on site and the nearest village (Oosterhout) has two shops. The nearest supermarket is in Elst (4 km).

Special offers
Many activities, such as children's clubs, are included in the price.

You might like to know
The site prides itself on its quiet and friendly atmosphere, which makes it particularly popular with nature lovers and visitors seeking a restful holiday, as well as cyclists, hikers and fishermen.

☐ Environmental accreditation
☐ Reduced energy/water consumption policy
☑ Recycling and reusing policy
☑ Information about walking and cycling
☑ Footpaths within 500 m. of the site
☑ Fishing within 1 km.
☐ Riding or pony trekking within 1 km.
☑ Direct river or lake access
☑ Within 10 km. of an area of outstanding natural beauty or national park
☑ Wildlife haven (on site/within 1 km)
☑ Public transport
☑ Dogs welcome

Facilities: Three sanitary buildings are modern and well maintained with free hot showers and facilities for babies. Laundry facilities. Snack bar. Playground with trampoline and open-air chess.

Open: 9 April - 9 October.

Directions: The site is 9 km. northwest of Nijmegen, on the northern banks of the Waal. GPS: 51.87585, 5.80752

Charges guide

Per unit incl. 5 persons and electricity	€ 24,50
dog	€ 3,00

Vikær Diernæs Strand Camping

Dundelum 29, Diernæs, DK-6100 Haderslev (Sønderjylland)
t: 74 57 54 64   e: info@vikaercamp.dk
alanrogers.com/DK2022   www.vikaercamp.dk

Accommodation: ☑Pitch ☑Mobile home/chalet ☐ Hotel/B&B ☐ Apartment

The warm welcome at Vikær Diernæs will start your holiday off in the right way. This family site in Southern Jutland lies in beautiful surroundings, right on the Diernæs Bugt beaches – ideal for both active campers and relaxation seekers. The attractively laid out site has 330 grass pitches (210 for touring units), all with 10/16A electricity and separated by low hedges. Access is from long, gravel lanes. The upper part of the site provides 40 newly developed, fully serviced pitches with electricity, water, sewerage, TV aerial point and internet. From these, and from the front pitches on the lower fields, there are marvellous views over the Diernæs Bugt. The site is next to a Blue Flag beach providing safe swimming. For the active there are several routes for walking and cycling and, of course, sea fishing trips are possible. In the area are a newly developed swamp nature reserve, Schackenborg Castle and the battlefields of Dybbøl Banke.

You might like to know

The campsite has direct access to a beautiful sandy beach where children can have hours of fun.

- ☐ Environmental accreditation
- ☐ Reduced energy/water consumption policy
- ☑ Recycling and reusing policy
- ☑ Information about walking and cycling
- ☐ Footpaths within 500 m. of the site
- ☑ Fishing within 1 km.
- ☐ Riding or pony trekking within 1 km.
- ☐ Direct river or lake access
- ☐ Within 10 km. of an area of outstanding natural beauty or national park
- ☑ Wildlife haven (on site/within 1 km)
- ☐ Public transport
- ☑ Dogs welcome

Facilities: Three modern toilet blocks with washbasins in cabins and controllable hot showers. Family shower rooms. Children's section. Baby room. En-suite facilities for disabled visitors. Laundry. Campers' kitchen. Motorcaravan services. Shop (Thursday-Sunday 07.30-21.00). Playground. Minigolf. Fishing. Archery. Watersports and boat launching. Petanque. TV room. Play house with Lego and Play Station. Daily activities for children in high season. Torch useful. English is spoken. Off site: Riding 2 km. Golf 30 minutes.

Open: Week before Easter - mid October.

Directions: From German/Danish border follow E45 north. Take exit 69 and follow to Hoptrup. From Hoptrup follow to Diernæs and Diernæs Strand. GPS: 55.15029, 9.4969

Charges guide

Per person	DKK 67
child (under 12 yrs)	DKK 45
pitch	DKK 25 - 60
electricity	DKK 28
dog	DKK 10

DENMARK – Jelling

Fårup Sø Camping

Fårupvej 58, DK-7300 Jelling (Vejle)
t: 75 87 13 44 e: faarup-soe@dk-camp.dk
alanrogers.com/DK2048 www.dk-camp.dk/faarup-soe

Accommodation: ☑Pitch ☑Mobile home/chalet ☐ Hotel/B&B ☐ Apartment

This site was originally set up in the woodlands of Jelling Skov where local farmers each had their own plot. Owned since January 2004 by the Dutch/Danish Albring family, this is a rural location on the Fårup Lake. Many of the trees have now been removed to give the site a welcoming, open feel. Fårup Sø Camping has 250 grassy pitches, mostly on terraces (from top to bottom the height difference is 53 m). The 35 newest terraced pitches provide beautiful views of the countryside and the Fårup lake. There are 200 pitches for touring units, most with 10A electricity, and some tent pitches without electricity. A new heated swimming pool, a whirlpool and an indoor play area have been added. Next to the top toilet block is a barbecue area with a terrace and good views. A neighbour rents out water bikes and takes high season excursions onto the lake with a real Viking Ship. This family site is ideal for those who want to enjoy a relaxed holiday on the lakeside beaches or go walking or cycling through the surrounding countryside.

You might like to know

Why not visit Legoland in the country that invented it? It is only 20 km. from this site.

☐ Environmental accreditation
☐ Reduced energy/water consumption policy
☑ Recycling and reusing policy
☑ Information about walking and cycling
☐ Footpaths within 500 m. of the site
☑ Fishing within 1 km.
☑ Riding or pony trekking within 1 km.
☑ Direct river or lake access
☐ Within 10 km. of an area of outstanding natural beauty or national park
☑ Wildlife haven (on site/within 1 km)
☐ Public transport
☑ Dogs welcome

Facilities: One modern and one older toilet block have British style toilets, open style washbasins and controllable hot showers. Family shower rooms. Baby room. Facilities for disabled visitors. Laundry. Campers' kitchen. Motorcaravan services. Shop (bread to order). New heated swimming pool (min. 25 degrees) and whirlpool (free of charge). Indoor play area. Playgrounds. Minigolf. Games room. Pony riding. Lake with fishing, watersports and Viking ship. Activities for children (high season). Internet. Off site: Golf and riding 2 km. Lion Park 8 km. Boat launching 10 km. Legoland 20 km.

Open: 1 April - 30 September.

Directions: From Vejle take the 28 road towards Billund. In Skibet turn right towards Fårup Sø, Jennum and Jelling and follow the signs to Fårup Sø. GPS: 55.73614, 9.41777

Charges guide

Per person	DKK 61
child (3-11 yrs)	DKK 35
pitch	DKK 15 - 35
electricity	DKK 28

Holmens Camping

Klostervej 148, DK-8680 Ry (Århus)
t: 86 89 17 62   e: info@holmens-camping.dk
alanrogers.com/DK2080   www.holmens-camping.dk

Accommodation: ☑Pitch ☑Mobile home/chalet   ☐ Hotel/B&B   ☐ Apartment

Holmens Camping lies between Silkeborg and Skanderborg in a very beautiful part of Denmark. The site is close to the waters of the Gudensø and Rye Møllesø lakes which are used for boating and canoeing. Walking and cycling are also popular activities. Holmens has 225 grass touring pitches, partly terraced and divided by young trees and shrubs. The site itself is surrounded by mature trees. Almost all the pitches have 6A electricity and vary in size between 70-100 sq.m. A small tent field is close to the lake, mainly used by those who like to travel by canoe. The lake is suitable for swimming but the site also has an attractive pool complex. This comprises two circular pools linked by a bridge and a paddling pool with water canon. There are plenty of opportunities for activities including boat hire on the lake and fishing (the site has its own fishing pond). Both Skanderborg and Silkeborg are worth a visit and in Ry you can attend the Skt. Hans party which takes place at midsummer.

You might like to know

Canoes can be hired and a trip along the river makes a day out with a difference.

☐ Environmental accreditation
☐ Reduced energy/water consumption policy
☑ Recycling and reusing policy
☑ Information about walking and cycling
☑ Footpaths within 500 m. of the site
☑ Fishing within 1 km.
☐ Riding or pony trekking within 1 km.
☑ Direct river or lake access
☐ Within 10 km. of an area of outstanding natural beauty or national park
☑ Wildlife haven (on site/within 1 km)
☐ Public transport
☑ Dogs welcome

Facilities: One traditional and one modern toilet block have washbasins (open and in cabins) and controllable hot showers (on payment). En-suite facilities with toilet, basin, shower. Baby room. Excellent facilities for disabled visitors. Laundry. Campers' kitchen. Small shop. Covered pool with jet stream and paddling pool with water canon. Finnish sauna, solarium, massage and fitness facilities (charged). Pool bar. Extensive games room. Playground. Tennis. Minigolf. Fishing. Bicycle hire. Boat rental. Large units are not accepted. Off site: Riding 2 km. Golf 14 km.

Open: 16 March - 29 September.

Directions: Going north on E45, take exit 52 at Skanderborg turning west on 445 road towards Ry. In Ry follow the site signs.
GPS: 56.07607, 9.76549

Charges guide

Per person	DKK 62 - 73
child (3-11 yrs)	DKK 35 - 40
pitch	DKK 20

Odda Camping

Borsto, N-5750 Odda (Hordaland)
t: 41 32 16 10 e: post@oppleve.no
alanrogers.com/NO2320 www.oppleve.no

Accommodation: ☑ Pitch ☑ Mobile home/chalet ☐ Hotel/B&B ☐ Apartment

Bordered by the Folgefonna glacier to the west and the Hardangervidda plateau to the east and south, Odda is an industrial town with electro-chemical enterprises based on zinc mining and hydro-electric power. This site has been attractively developed on the town's southern outskirts. It is spread over 2.5 acres of flat, mature woodland, which is divided into small clearings by massive boulders. Access is by well tended tarmac roads which wind their way among the trees and boulders. There are 55 tourist pitches including 36 with electricity. The site fills up in the evenings and can be crowded with facilities stretched from the end of June to early August. The site is just over a kilometre from the centre of town, on the shores of the Sandvin lake (good salmon and trout fishing) and on the minor road leading up the Buar Valley to the Buar glacier, Vidfoss Falls and Folgefonna ice cap. It is possible to walk to the ice face but in the later stages this is quite hard going!

You might like to know

Teenagers will love the challenge and excitement of paintball, where they can have hours of fun with friends.

- ☐ Environmental accreditation
- ☑ Reduced energy/water consumption policy
- ☑ Recycling and reusing policy
- ☑ Information about walking and cycling
- ☑ Footpaths within 500 m. of the site
- ☐ Fishing within 1 km.
- ☐ Riding or pony trekking within 1 km.
- ☐ Direct river or lake access
- ☐ Within 10 km. of an area of outstanding natural beauty or national park
- ☑ Wildlife haven (on site/within 1 km)
- ☐ Public transport
- ☐ Dogs welcome

Facilities: A single timber building at the entrance houses the reception office and the simple, but clean, sanitary facilities which provide for each sex, two WCs, one hot shower (on payment) and three open washbasins. A new building provides additional unisex toilets, showers and laundry facilities. Small kitchen with dishwashing facilities. Mini shop. Off site: Town facilities close.

Open: All year.

Directions: Site is on the southern outskirts of Odda, signed off road to Buar, with a well marked access. GPS: 60.05320, 6.54380

Charges guide

Per person	NOK 10
tent and car	NOK 110
caravan or motorcaravan	NOK 130
electricity	NOK 40

No credit cards.

NORWAY – Andenes

Andenes Camping

Storgata 53, N-8483 Andenes (Nordland)
t: 76 14 14 12   e: camping@whalesafari.no
alanrogers.com/NO2428   www.andenescamping.no

Accommodation: ☑Pitch ☑Mobile home/chalet ☐ Hotel/B&B ☐ Apartment

Lying on the exposed west coast of Andøy between the quiet main road and white sandy beaches, this site has an exceptional location for the midnight sun. Extremely popular, offering mountain and ocean views, it is only three kilometres from the base of Whalesafari and Andenes town. There is space for an unspecified number of touring units and you park where you like. With only 20 places with 16A electricity connections, it is advisable to arrive by mid-afternoon. Late arrivals may pitch and pay later when reception opens. Level areas of grass with some hardstanding can be found on gently sloping ground. Visitors come to Andenes for the opportunities to see whales at close quarters. Whalesafari is deemed the world's largest, most successful Arctic whale watching operation for the general public. It is worth driving north to the site along the road which follows the west coast, a National Tourist road because of the areas outstanding natural beauty it passes through.

You might like to know
The village of Andenes is around 2 km. from the campsite and has a good range of amenities.

☐ Environmental accreditation
☑ Reduced energy/water consumption policy
☑ Recycling and reusing policy
☑ Information about walking and cycling
☑ Footpaths within 500 m. of the site
☐ Fishing within 1 km.
☐ Riding or pony trekking within 1 km.
☐ Direct river or lake access
☐ Within 10 km. of an area of outstanding natural beauty or national park
☑ Wildlife haven (on site/within 1 km)
☐ Public transport
☑ Dogs welcome

Facilities: One building houses separate sex sanitary facilities providing for each two toilets, two showers (10 NOK) with curtain to keep clothes dry and three washbasins. In each, one toilet is suitable for disabled visitors and includes a washbasin. The reception building houses a well equipped kitchen, a large sitting/dining room, 2 showers, WC and washbasin. Laundry facilities. Motorcaravan service point. Chemical disposal (charged 30 NOK). Picnic tables. Swings for children. WiFi (free). Off site: Well stocked supermarket 250 m. On approach to town a garage, caravan dealer and another supermarket. From nearby village of Bleik (8 km), trips are available for deep sea fishing and to Bleiksøya one of Norway's most famous bird cliffs with 80,000 pairs of puffins and 6,000 kittiwakes. Whale safari 3 km. Guided walks. Kayaking.

Open: 1 June - 30 September.

Directions: Either take the scenic roads 946 and 947 on the west side of Andøy north or to the east road 82, site is on left 250 m. from where 947 rejoins the 82, 3 km. before Andenes. The scenic west route is about 9 km. further. GPS: 69.30411, 16.06641

Charges guide

Per unit incl. electricity	NOK 200
car	NOK 100

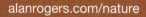

Trollveggen Camping

Horgheimseidet, N-6300 Åndalsnes (Møre og Romsdal)
t: **71 22 37 00** e: **post@trollveggen.no**
alanrogers.com/NO2452 www.trollveggen.no

Accommodation: ☑Pitch ☑Mobile home/chalet ☐ Hotel/B&B ☐ Apartment

The location of this site provides a unique experience – it is set at the foot of the famous vertical cliff of Trollveggen (the Troll Wall), which is Europe's highest vertical mountain face. The site is pleasantly laid out in terraces with level grass pitches. The facility block, four cabins and the reception are all very attractively built with grass roofs. Beside the river is an attractive barbecue area where barbecue parties are sometimes arranged. This site is a must for people who love nature. The site is surrounded by the Troll Peaks and the Romsdalshorn Mountains with the rapid river of Rauma flowing by. Here in the beautiful valley of Romsdalen you have the ideal starting point for trips to many outstanding attractions such as 'The Troll Road' to Geiranger or to the Mandalsfossen waterfalls. In the mountains there are nature trails of various lengths and difficulties. The campsite owners are happy to help you with information. The town of Åndalsnes is 10 km. away and has a long tourism tradition as a place to visit.

Special offers

Stay 7 nights or more and get 10% discount on camping, or 5% discount on the cabins.

You might like to know

Trollveggen Camping offers a unique nature experience, with its spectacular view of the Troll Wall. The Romsdalen Alps is a must for hikers, climbers and everyone who loves wild and beautiful scenery.

☐ Environmental accreditation
☐ Reduced energy/water consumption policy
☐ Recycling and reusing policy
☑ Information about walking and cycling
☑ Footpaths within 500 m. of the site
☑ Fishing within 1 km.
☐ Riding or pony trekking within 1 km.
☑ Direct river or lake access
☑ Within 10 km. of an area of outstanding natural beauty or national park
☑ Wildlife haven (on site/within 1 km)
☑ Public transport
☑ Dogs welcome

Facilities: One heated toilet block provides washbasins, some in cubicles, and showers on payment. Family room with baby bath and changing mat, plus facilities for disabled visitors. Communal kitchen with cooking rings, small ovens, fridge and sinks (free hot water). Laundry facilities. Motorcaravan service point. Barbecue area (covered). Playground. Duck pond. Off site: Climbing, glacier walking and hiking. Fjord fishing. Sightseeing trips. The Troll Road. Mardalsfossen (waterfall). Geiranger and Åndalsnes.

Open: 10 May - 20 September.

Directions: Site is located on the E136 road, 10 km. south of Åndalsnes. It is signed. GPS: 62.49444, 7.758333

Charges guide

Per unit incl. 2 persons and electricity	NOK 190 - 210
extra person (over 4 yrs)	NOK 10

No credit cards.

NORWAY – Averoy

Skjerneset Bryggecamping

Ekkilsoya, N-6530 Averoy (Møre og Romsdal)
t: **71 51 18 94** e: info@skjerneset.com
alanrogers.com/NO2490 www.skjerneset.com

Accommodation: ☑ Pitch ☑ Mobile home/chalet ☐ Hotel/B&B ☑ Apartment

Uniquely centred around a working fishing quay set in an idyllic bay, Skjerneset Camping has been developed by the Otterlei family to give visitors an historical insight into this industry. It steps back in time in all but its facilities and offers 20 boats to hire and organised trips on a real fishing boat. Found on the tiny island of Ekkilsøya off Averøy, there is space for 30 caravans or motorcaravans on gravel hardstandings landscaped into rocks and trees, each individually shaped and sized and all having electricity connections (10/16A). There are grassy areas for tents on the upper terraces and six fully equipped cabins. Although the fishing industry here has declined, it is still the dominant activity. The old Klippfisk warehouse is now a fascinating 'fisherimuseum' and also houses the main sanitary installations and reception. It encompasses a large kitchen, laundry, several lounges with satellite TV and others for those who prefer to make their own entertainment, and five small four-bed apartments.

You might like to know

Why not try some relaxing fishing? The campsite will be happy to arrange a boat for you.

- ☐ Environmental accreditation
- ☑ Reduced energy/water consumption policy
- ☑ Recycling and reusing policy
- ☑ Information about walking and cycling
- ☑ Footpaths within 500 m. of the site
- ☑ Fishing within 1 km.
- ☐ Riding or pony trekking within 1 km.
- ☐ Direct river or lake access
- ☐ Within 10 km. of an area of outstanding natural beauty or national park
- ☑ Wildlife haven (on site/within 1 km)
- ☐ Public transport
- ☐ Dogs welcome

Facilities: Unisex sanitary facilities are heated, but basic and include washbasins in cubicles. Two new sanitary blocks. Kitchen. Small laundry. Motorcaravan service point. Kiosk for basic packet foods, crisps, ices, sweets, postcards etc. Satellite TV. Motor boat hire. Organised sea fishing or sightseeing trips in the owner's sea-going boat, and for non anglers who want a fish supper, fresh fish are usually available on site.

Open: All year.

Directions: Site is on the little island of Ekkilsøya which is reached via a side road running west from the main Rv 64 road, 1.5 km. south of Bremsnes. GPS: 63.08135, 7.59612

Charges guide

Per person	NOK 150
pitch	NOK 250 - 500
electricity	NOK 25

No credit cards.

Neset Camping

N-4741 Byglandsfjord (Aust-Agder)
t: 37 93 42 55 e: post@neset.no
alanrogers.com/NO2610 www.neset.no

Accommodation: ☑Pitch ☑Mobile home/chalet ☐ Hotel/B&B ☐ Apartment

On a semi-promontory on the shores of the 40 km. long Byglandsfjord, Neset is a good centre for activities or as a stop en route north from the ferry port of Kristiansand (from England or Denmark). Neset is situated on well kept grassy meadows by the lake shore with the water on three sides and the road on the fourth, and provides 200 unmarked pitches with electricity and cable TV available. The main building houses reception, a small shop and a restaurant with fine views over the water. This is a well run, friendly site where one could spend an active few days. Byglandsfjord offers good fishing (mainly trout) and the area has marked trails for cycling, riding or walking in an area famous for its minerals.

You might like to know

Mountaineering courses are available. You can also go in search of various minerals along the Evje Mineral Path.

☐ Environmental accreditation
☐ Reduced energy/water consumption policy
☐ Recycling and reusing policy
☑ Information about walking and cycling
☑ Footpaths within 500 m. of the site
☑ Fishing within 1 km.
☐ Riding or pony trekking within 1 km.
☑ Direct river or lake access
☐ Within 10 km. of an area of outstanding natural beauty or national park
☐ Wildlife haven (on site/within 1 km)
☐ Public transport
☑ Dogs welcome

Facilities: Three modern sanitary blocks which can be heated, all with comfortable hot showers (some on payment), washing up facilities (metered hot water) and a kitchen. Restaurant and takeaway (15/6-15/8). Shop (1/5-1/10). Campers' kitchen. Playground. Lake swimming, boating and fishing. Excellent new barbecue area and hot tub. Bicycle, canoe and pedalo hire. Climbing, rafting and canoeing courses arranged (including trips to see beavers and elk). Cross-country skiing possible in winter. Off site: Rock climbing wall. Marked forest trails.

Open: All year.

Directions: Site is on route 9, 2.5 km. north of the town of Byglandsfjord on the eastern shores of the lake. GPS: 58.68848, 7.80132

Charges guide

Per person	NOK 10
pitch	NOK 160
child (5-12 yrs)	NOK 5
electricity	NOK 30

Röstånga Camping & Bad

Blinkarpsvägen 3, S-260 24 Röstånga (Skåne Län)
t: 043 591 064 e: nystrand@msn.com
alanrogers.com/SW2630 www.rostangacamping.se

Accommodation: ☑Pitch ☑Mobile home/chalet ☐ Hotel/B&B ☐ Apartment

Beside the Söderåsen National Park, this scenic campsite has its own fishing lake and many activities for the whole family. There are 136 large, level, grassy pitches with electricity (10A) and a quiet area for tents with a view over the fishing lake. The tent area has its own service building and several barbecue places. A large holiday home and 14 pleasant cabins are available to rent all year round. A pool complex adjacent to the site provides a 50 m. swimming pool, three children's pools and a water slide, all heated during peak season. Activities are arranged on the site in high season, including a children's club with exciting activities such as treasure hunts and gold panning, and for adults, aquarobics, Nordic walking and tennis. The Söderåsen National Park offers hiking and bicycle trails. The friendly staff will be happy to help you to plan interesting excursions in the area.

Special offers
Free entry to the zoo and swimming pool complex.

You might like to know
Located on the southern slope of Söderåsen National Park, one of Sweden's most visited tourist attractions, which has its own unique beauty and an abundance of flora and fauna.

☐ Environmental accreditation
☑ Reduced energy/water consumption policy
☑ Recycling and reusing policy
☑ Information about walking and cycling
☑ Footpaths within 500 m. of the site
☑ Fishing within 1 km.
☐ Riding or pony trekking within 1 km.
☑ Direct river or lake access
☑ Within 10 km. of an area of outstanding natural beauty or national park
☑ Wildlife haven (on site/within 1 km)
☐ Public transport
☐ Dogs welcome

Facilities: Four good, heated sanitary blocks with free hot water and facilities for babies and disabled visitors. Laundry with washing machines and dryers. Kitchen with cooking rings, oven and microwave. Motorcaravan service point. Small shop at reception. Bar, restaurant and takeaway. Minigolf. Tennis. Fitness trail. Fishing. Canoe hire. Children's club. WiFi. Off site: Swimming pool complex adjacent to site (free for campers as is a visit to the zoo). Many golf courses nearby. Motor racing track at Ring Knutstorp 8 km.

Open: 21 April - 2 October.

Directions: From Malmö: drive towards Lund and follow road no. 108 to Röstånga. From Stockholm: turn off at Östra Ljungby and take road no. 13 to Röstånga. In Röstånga drive through the village on road no. 108 and follow the signs. GPS: 55.996583, 13.28005

Charges guide

Per unit incl. 2 persons and electricity	SEK 25 - 33

FINLAND – Virrat

Camping Lakari

Lakarintie 405, FIN-34800 Virrat (Häme)
t: 034 758 639 e: lakari@virtainmatkailu.fi
alanrogers.com/FI2830 www.virtainmatkailu.fi

Accommodation: ☑Pitch ☑Mobile home/chalet ☐ Hotel/B&B ☐ Apartment

The peace and tranquillity of the beautiful natural surroundings are the main attractions at this vast (18-hectare) campsite which is located on a narrow piece of land between two lakes. This site is a must if you want to get away from it all. There are a variety of cabins to rent, some with their own beach and jetty! Marked pitches for tents and caravans are beside the beach or in little meadows in the forest. You pick your own place. Site amenities include a café and a beach sauna. This is a spectacular landscape with deep gorges and steep lakeside cliffs. There is a nature trail from the site to the lakes of Toriseva and pleasant excursions to the Esteri Zoo and the village shop in Keskinen. The Helvetinjärvi National Park is nearby. Facilities at the site are rather basic but very clean and well kept. This is a glorious place for a nature loving tourist looking to relax.

You might like to know
The peaceful setting of this site offers visitors a truly tranquil experience.

- ☐ Environmental accreditation
- ☑ Reduced energy/water consumption policy
- ☑ Recycling and reusing policy
- ☑ Information about walking and cycling
- ☐ Footpaths within 500 m. of the site
- ☑ Fishing within 1 km.
- ☐ Riding or pony trekking within 1 km.
- ☑ Direct river or lake access
- ☐ Within 10 km. of an area of outstanding natural beauty or national park
- ☑ Wildlife haven (on site/within 1 km)
- ☐ Public transport
- ☑ Dogs welcome

Facilities: Two toilet blocks, basic but clean and well kept, include toilets, washbasins and showers. Free hot water. Chemical disposal and motorcaravan service point. Covered campers' kitchen with fridge, cooking rings and oven. Washing machine. Small shop and caféteria. TV. Fishing. Bicycle hire. Off site: Golf 1 km. Riding 5 km.

Open: 1 May - 30 September.

Directions: Site is 7 km. south of Virrat on road 66. Follow signs.
GPS: 62.209817, 23.837767

Charges guide

Per unit incl. 2 persons and electricity	€ 22,00
extra person	€ 3,00
child	€ 1,50

Camping Haapasaaren Lomakylä

Haapasaarentie 5, FIN-34600 Ruovesi (Häme)
t: 044 080 0290 e: lomakyla@haapasaari.fi
alanrogers.com/FI2840 www.haapasaari.fi

Accommodation: ☑ Pitch ☑ Mobile home/chalet ☐ Hotel/B&B ☐ Apartment

Haapasaaren is located on Lake Näsijärvi, around 70 km. north of Tampere in south western Finland. This is a well equipped site with a café and restaurant, a traditional Finnish outside dancing area and, of course, plenty of saunas! Rowing boats, canoes, cycles and, during the winter months, sleds are all available for rent. Fishing is very popular here. Pitches are grassy and of a good size. There is also a good range of accommodation to rent, including holiday cottages with saunas. The cosy restaurant has an attractive terrace and fine views across the lake. Haapasaaren's friendly owners organise a series of guided tours throughout the year. These include hiking and nature treks, berry and mushroom picking, and, during the winter, ice fishing and cross-country skiing. Helvetinjärvi National Park is one of the most dramatic areas of western Finland, made up of deep gorges and dense forests. There is a rich population of birds and occasionally even brown bears and lynx can be seen here.

You might like to know

Camping Haapasaaren is the ideal place to relax surrounded by nature. In fact, it is an island surrounded by shimmering blue water.

- ☐ Environmental accreditation
- ☑ Reduced energy/water consumption policy
- ☑ Recycling and reusing policy
- ☑ Information about walking and cycling
- ☑ Footpaths within 500 m. of the site
- ☑ Fishing within 1 km.
- ☐ Riding or pony trekking within 1 km.
- ☑ Direct river or lake access
- ☑ Within 10 km. of an area of outstanding natural beauty or national park
- ☑ Wildlife haven (on site/within 1 km)
- ☐ Public transport
- ☑ Dogs welcome

Facilities: Café. Restaurant. Direct lake access. Saunas. Fishing. Minigolf. Boat and canoe hire. Bicycle hire. Guided tours. Play area. Tourist information. Chalets for rent. Internet access. Off site: Walking and cycle routes. Boat trips. Helvetinjärvi National Park.

Open: All year.

Directions: From Helsinki, head north on the E12 motorway to Tampere and then northeast on N63-9 to Orivesi. Then, continue north on route 66 to Ruovesi and follow signs to the site. GPS: 61.99413, 24.069843

Charges guide

Per unit incl. 2 persons and electricity	€ 25,00
extra person	€ 4,00
child (under 15 yrs)	€ 2,00

Ukonjärvi Camping

Ukonjärventi 141, FIN-99801 Ivalo (Lapland)
t: **016 667 501**   e: **nuttu@ukolo.fi**
alanrogers.com/FI2995   www.ukolo.fi

Accommodation: ☑ Pitch ☑ Mobile home/chalet ☐ Hotel/B&B ☐ Apartment

Ukonjärvi Camping lies on the banks of Lake Inari, situated in a forested area alongside a nature reserve. It is a quiet, peaceful site, ideal for rest and relaxation. Thirty touring pitches have electricity and are surrounded by pine and beech trees. Cottages are available to rent. A bar and restaurant are located at reception; a range of local dishes are produced including reindeer casserole. There is also a barbecue hut, located in the centre of the site, if you prefer to cook your own food. A climb up to the nearby viewpoint offers spectacular views over the lake – you can even see over to Russia. The lake also provides plenty of opportunities for boating and fishing.

You might like to know
This must surely be one of the few opportunities to take a holiday north of the Arctic Circle!

- ☐ Environmental accreditation
- ☐ Reduced energy/water consumption policy
- ☐ Recycling and reusing policy
- ☑ Information about walking and cycling
- ☑ Footpaths within 500 m. of the site
- ☑ Fishing within 1 km.
- ☐ Riding or pony trekking within 1 km.
- ☑ Direct river or lake access
- ☑ Within 10 km. of an area of outstanding natural beauty or national park
- ☑ Wildlife haven (on site/within 1 km)
- ☐ Public transport
- ☑ Dogs welcome

Facilities: Sanitary block includes toilets and showers. Laundry and campers' kitchen. Lakeside sauna (charged). Bar and restaurant. Barbecue hut with logs. Small beach. Fishing and boating on lake. TV room. WiFi.
Off site: Tankavaaran Kansainvalinen Kulamuseo, a gold mining experience where you can try gold panning, keeping what you find! The Northern Lapland Centre and the Sami Museum, displaying cultural and natural history exhibitions.

Open: May - September.

Directions: Ukonjärvi Camping is 11 km. north of Ivalo on road 4. Look for signs to Lake Inari viewpoint; site is about 1 km. down a narrow road (signed). GPS: 68.73687, 27.47687

Charges guide

Per person	€ 3,50
child	€ 2,50
pitch incl. electricity	€ 19,00

Camping & Freizeitpark LuxOase

Arnsdorfer Strasse 1, Kleinröhrsdorf, D-01900 Dresden (Saxony)
t: 035 952 56666 e: info@luxoase.de
alanrogers.com/DE3833 www.luxoase.de

Accommodation: ☑Pitch ☑Mobile home/chalet ☐Hotel/B&B ☐Apartment

This is a well organised and quiet site located just north of Dresden with easy access from the autobahn. The site has very good facilities and is arranged on grassland beside a lake. There is access from the site to the lake through a gate. Although the site is fairly open, trees do provide shade in some areas. There are 138 large touring pitches (plus 50 seasonal in a separate area), marked by bushes or posts on generally flat or slightly sloping grass. All have 10/16A electricity and 100 have water and drainage. At the entrance is an area of hardstanding (with electricity) for late arrivals. The main entrance building houses the amenities. You may swim, fish or use inflatables in the lake. A wide entertainment programme is organised for children in high season. There are many interesting places to visit apart from Dresden and Meissen, with the fascinating National Park Sächsische Schweiz (Saxon Switzerland) on the border with the Czech Republic offering some spectacular scenery. A member of Leading Campings Group.

You might like to know

The campsite organises a number of excursions allowing you to make the most of your visit to this beautiful region.

- ☐ Environmental accreditation
- ☐ Reduced energy/water consumption policy
- ☑ Recycling and reusing policy
- ☑ Information about walking and cycling
- ☐ Footpaths within 500 m. of the site
- ☑ Fishing within 1 km.
- ☑ Riding or pony trekking within 1 km.
- ☑ Direct river or lake access
- ☐ Within 10 km. of an area of outstanding natural beauty or national park
- ☑ Wildlife haven (on site/within 1 km)
- ☑ Public transport
- ☑ Dogs welcome

Facilities: A well equipped building provides modern, heated facilities with private cabins, a family room, baby room, units for disabled visitors and two bathrooms for hire. Jacuzzi. Kitchen. Gas supplies. Motorcaravan services. Shop and bar (1/3-31/12) plus restaurant (15/3-31/12). Bicycle hire. Lake swimming. Sports field. Fishing. Play area. Sauna. Train, bus and theatre tickets from reception. Internet point. WiFi. Minigolf. Fitness room. Regular guided bus trips to Dresden, Prague etc. Off site: Riding next door (lessons available). Public transport to Dresden 1 km. Golf 7.5 km. Nearby Dinosaur park, zoo and indoor karting etc.

Open: 1 March - 31 December.

Directions: Site is 17 km. northeast of Dresden. From the A4 (Dresden - Görlitz) take exit 85 (Pulnitz) and travel south towards Radeberg. Pass through Leppersdorf and site is signed to the left. Follow signs for Kleinröhrsdorf and camping. Site is 4 km. from the autobahn exit. GPS: 51.120401, 13.980103

Charges guide

Per unit incl. 2 persons and electricity	€ 20,10 - € 29,50
extra person	€ 5,00 - € 7,80
child (3-15 yrs)	€ 2,50 - € 4,50

CZECH REPUBLIC – Dolnl Branná

Holiday Park Lisci Farma

Dolni Branna 350, CZ-54362 Dolni Branná (Vychodocesky)
t: 499 421 473   e: info@liscifarma.cz
alanrogers.com/CZ4590   www.liscifarma.cz

Accommodation: ☑Pitch ☑Mobile home/chalet ☐ Hotel/B&B ☐ Apartment

This is truly an excellent site that could be in Western Europe considering its amenities, pitches and welcome. However, Lisci Farma retains a pleasant Czech atmosphere. In the winter months, when local skiing is available, snow chains are essential. The 260 pitches are fairly flat, although the terrain is slightly sloping and some pitches are terraced. There is shade and some pitches have hardstanding. The site is well equipped for the whole family with its adventure playground offering trampolines for children, archery, beach volleyball, Russian bowling and an outdoor bowling court for older youngsters. A beautiful sandy, lakeside beach is 800 m. from the entrance. The more active can go paragliding or rock climbing, with experienced people to guide you. Excursions to Prague are organised and, if all the sporting possibilities are not enough, children can take part in the activities of the entertainment team, while you are walking or cycling or enjoying live music at the Fox Saloon.

You might like to know

After a busy day, why not relax body and mind with one of the soothing massages available on site?

☐ Environmental accreditation
☐ Reduced energy/water consumption policy
☐ Recycling and reusing policy
☑ Information about walking and cycling
☐ Footpaths within 500 m. of the site
☑ Fishing within 1 km.
☐ Riding or pony trekking within 1 km.
☑ Direct river or lake access
☐ Within 10 km. of an area of outstanding natural beauty or national park
☑ Wildlife haven (on site/within 1 km)
☑ Public transport
☑ Dogs welcome

Facilities: Two good sanitary blocks, one new in 2005 near the entrance and another modern block next to the hotel, both include toilets, washbasins and spacious, controllable showers (on payment). Child size toilets and baby room. Toilet for disabled visitors. Sauna and massage. Launderette with sinks, hot water and a washing machine. Shop (15/6-15/9). Mini-market. Bar/snack bar with pool table. Restaurant. Games room. Swimming pool (6x12 m). Adventure style playground on grass with climbing wall. Trampolines. Tennis. Minigolf. Archery. Russian bowling. Paragliding. Rock climbing. Bicycle hire. Entertainment programme. Excursions to Prague. Off site: Fishing and beach 800 m. Riding 2 km. Golf 5 km.

Open: 1 May - 30 September.

Directions: Follow road no. 14 from Liberec to Vrchlabi. At the roundabout turn in the direction of Prague and site is about 1.5 km. on the right. GPS: 50.61036, 15.60264

Charges guide

Per unit incl. 2 persons, 2 children and electricity	CZK 400 - 920
extra person	CZK 90 - 120
child (5-12 yrs)	CZK 35 - 59
dog	CZK 39 - 59

CZECH REPUBLIC – Frymburk

Camping Frymburk

Frymburk 184, CZ-38279 Frymburk (Jihocesky)
t: 380 735 284 e: info@campingfrymburk.cz
alanrogers.com/CZ4720 www.campingfrymburk.cz

Accommodation: ☑Pitch ☑Mobile home/chalet ☐Hotel/B&B ☐Apartment

Camping Frymburk is beautifully located on the Lipno lake in southern Bohemia and is an ideal site. From this site, activities could include walking, cycling, swimming, sailing, canoeing or rowing and afterwards you could relax in the small, cosy bar/restaurant. You could enjoy a real Czech meal in one of the restaurants in Frymburk or on site. The site has 170 level pitches on terraces (all with 6A electricity, some with hardstanding and 4 have private sanitary units) and from the lower terraces on the edge of the lake there are lovely views over the water to the woods on the opposite side. A ferry crosses the lake from Frymburk where one can walk or cycle in the woods. The Dutch owner, Mr Wilzing, will welcome the whole family, personally siting your caravan. Children will be entertained by 'Kidstown' and the site has a small beach.

You might like to know

Excursions from site include the UNESCO city Cesky Krumlov, castle Rozmberk and Hluboká nad Vltavou, Vítkuv Kámen.

- ☐ Environmental accreditation
- ☐ Reduced energy/water consumption policy
- ☑ Recycling and reusing policy
- ☑ Information about walking and cycling
- ☐ Footpaths within 500 m. of the site
- ☐ Fishing within 1 km.
- ☐ Riding or pony trekking within 1 km.
- ☑ Direct river or lake access
- ☐ Within 10 km. of an area of outstanding natural beauty or national park
- ☑ Wildlife haven (on site/within 1 km)
- ☑ Public transport
- ☑ Dogs welcome

Facilities: Three immaculate toilet blocks with toilets, washbasins, preset showers on payment and an en-suite bathroom with toilet, basin and shower. Facilities for disabled visitors. Launderette. Restaurant and bar (10/5-15/9). Motorcaravan services. Playground. Canoe, bicycle, pedalos, rowing boat and surfboard hire. Kidstown. Volleyball competitions. Rafting. Bus trips to Prague. Torches useful. Internet access and WiFi. Off site: Shops and restaurants in the village 900 m. Golf 7 km. Riding 20 km.

Open: 29 April - 1 October.

Directions: Take exit 114 at Passau in Germany (near the Austrian border) towards Freyung in the Czech Republic. Continue on this road till Philipsreut. From there follow the no. 4 road (Vimperk). Turn right a few kilometres after the border towards Volary on no. 141 road. From Volary follow the no. 163 road to Horni Plana, Cerna and Frymburk. Site is on the 163 road, right after village. GPS: 48.655947, 14.170239

Charges guide

Per unit incl. 2 persons and electricity	CZK 460 - 810
extra person	CZK 80 - 130
child (under 12 yrs)	CZK60 - 90

No credit cards.

Been to any good campsites lately?
We have

You'll find them here...

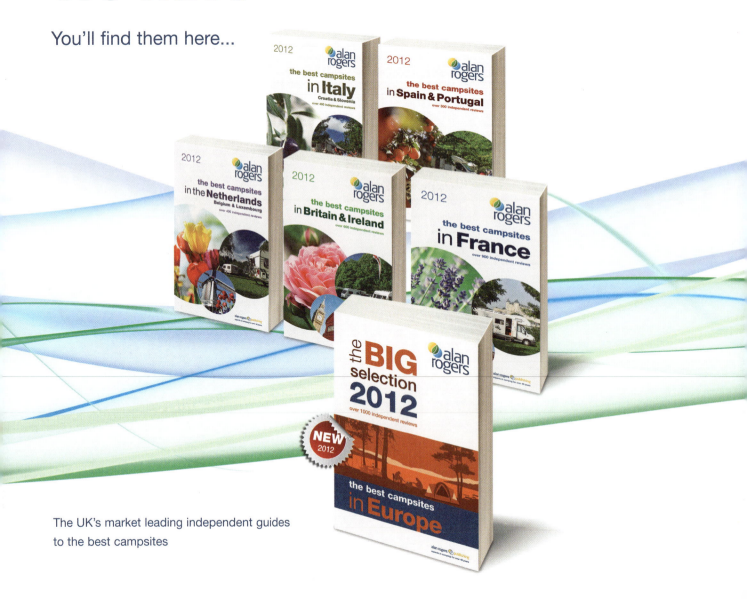

The UK's market leading independent guides
to the best campsites

... also here...

101 great campsites, ideal for your specific hobby,
pastime or passion

Want independent campsite reviews at your fingertips?

You'll find them here...

Over 3,000 in-depth campsite reviews at **www.alanrogers.com**

...and even here...

NOW ON ANDROID TOO

alan rogers

Search | Featured | Map

England
Finland
France
Germany
Greece
Hungary
Ireland
Italy

alan rogers

02:10 PM

Search Campsites

England	411 >
Finland	11 >
France	1036 >
Germany	90 >
Greece	27 >
Hungary	31 >
Ireland	47 >

Search | Featured | Map | About

An exciting free app from iTunes, the Apple app store or the Android Market

Want to book your holiday on one of Europe's top campsites?

We can do it for you. No problem.

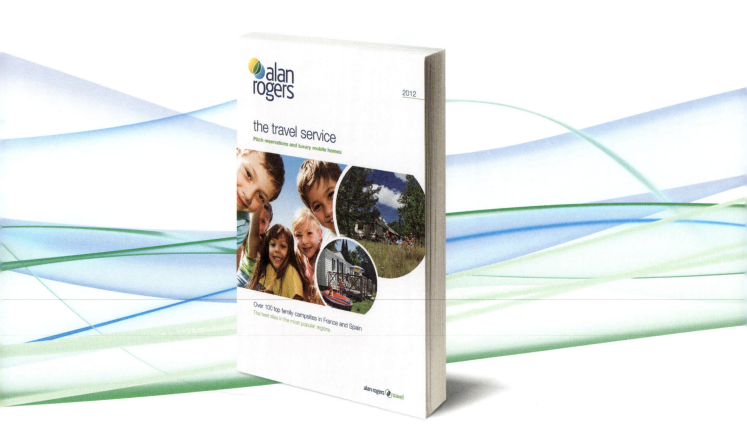

The best campsites in the most popular regions - we'll take care of everything

alan
rogers

Discover the best campsites in Europe
with Alan Rogers

alanrogers.com
01580 214000

index

index

index